Euripides: Alcestis

COMPANIONS TO GREEK AND ROMAN TRAGEDY

Series Editor: Thomas Harrison

Aeschylus: Agamemnon Barbara Goward
Aeschylus: Eumenides Robin Mitchell-Boyask
Aeschylus: Persians David Rosenbloom
Aeschylus: Prometheus Bound I. A. Ruffell
Aeschylus: Seven Against Thebes Isabelle Torrance
Aeschylus: Suppliants Thalia Papadopoulou
Euripides: Alcestis Niall W. Slater
Euripides: Bacchae Sophie Mills
Euripides: Heracles Emma Griffiths
Euripides: Hippolytus Sophie Mills
Euripides: Ion Lorna Swift
Euripides: Iphigenia at Aulis Pantelis Michelakis
Euripides: Medea William Allan
Euripides: Orestes Matthew Wright
Euripides: Phoenician Women Thalia Papadopoulou
Euripides: Suppliant Women Ian Storey
Euripides: Trojan Women Barbara Goff
Seneca: Phaedra Roland Mayer
Seneca: Thyestes Peter Davis
Sophocles: Ajax Jon Hesk
Sophocles: Electra Michael Lloyd
Sophocles: Oedipus at Colonus Adrian Kelly
Sophocles: Philoctetes Hanna Roisman
Sophocles: Women of Trachis Brad Levett

Euripides: Alcestis

Niall W. Slater

BLOOMSBURY
LONDON • NEW DELHI • NEW YORK • SYDNEY

Bloomsbury Academic
An imprint of Bloomsbury Publishing Plc

50 Bedford Square   1385 Broadway
London   New York
WC1B 3DP   NY 10018
UK   USA

www.bloomsbury.com

Bloomsbury is a registered trade mark of Bloomsbury Publishing Plc

First published 2013

© Niall W. Slater, 2013

Niall W. Slater has asserted his right under the Copyright, Designs and Patents Act, 1988, to be identified as Author of this work.

All rights reserved. No part of this publication may be reproduced or transmitted in any form or by any means, electronic or mechanical, including photocopying, recording, or any information storage or retrieval system, without prior permission in writing from the publishers.

No responsibility for loss caused to any individual or organization acting on or refraining from action as a result of the material in this publication can be accepted by Bloomsbury or the author.

British Library Cataloguing-in-Publication Data
A catalogue record for this book is available from the British Library.

ISBN: HB: 978-1-78093-472-3
PB: 978-1-78093-473-0
ePub: 978-1-78093-474-7
ePDF: 978-1-78093-475-4

Library of Congress Cataloging-in-Publication Data
A catalog record for this book is available from the Library of Congress.

Typeset by Fakenham Prepress Solutions, Fakenham, Norfolk NR21 8NN

Contents

Preface		ix
1	438 and All That	1
	The Myth(s)	8
	Production Conditions	10
2	The Action of the Play	15
	Prologue	15
	Parôdos	17
	Episode	18
	First Stasimon	19
	Episode	20
	Second Stasimon	23
	Episode	23
	Third Stasimon	25
	Episode	26
	Kommos	28
	Fourth Stasimon	29
	Episode and Exodos	29
3	Themes of the Play	31
	The House and the Door	32
	Husband and Wife	34
	Parents and Children	38
	Xenia, *Philia*, and *Charis*	41
	Life and Death	46
	Lament	47
	Fame and Infamy	50

	Doubles and Opposites	56
	Alcestis' Statue	57
	Marriage, Remarriage—and Silence	61
4	Afterlives of an Afterlife	67
	In Antiquity	67
	From Late Antiquity to the Renaissance	74
	From Shakespeare to the Nineteenth Century	77
	The Twentieth Century	86
	The Alcestiad	88
	Ted Hughes' *Alcestis*	91

Chronology	95
Abbreviations	98
Glossary	99
Guide to Further Reading	101
Texts, Commentaries, and Concordance	101
Translations	102
Adaptations	102
General Studies of Greek Tragedy and Reception	102
Books and Articles on *Alcestis*	103
Notes	105
Bibliography	127
Index	137

matri carissimae

Preface

I have loved the *Alcestis* ever since I first encountered it, for its many surprises as well as its beauties. This volume attempts to situate the play in its Athenian context as well as trace some of the widely varied fortunes *Alcestis* has enjoyed since then. The tone of the play and its emotional connection to its audience are the subject of wide and continuing controversy, and while I have a point of view on those questions, I hope the discussions here will have something to say to readers, performers, and audience members on a wide range of approaches.

The gestation of this volume has now exceeded that of Pliny's elephants (*Nat. Hist.* 8.10), and I am deeply indebted to Tom Harrison, the Series Editor, for his patience as well as his generous invitation and support. Deborah Blake and her successor, Charlotte Loveridge, have been of great help in bringing this to a conclusion. Audiences ranging from those at the 1993 Classical Association of the Middle West and South panel on performance (at the invitation of its president, Karelisa Hartigan) to the 2003 conference on Satyr Drama: Tragedy at Play (organized by G. W. M. Harrison) to the 2005 Wake Forest Institute of Literature have listened to and challenged some of these ideas. A blissful year at Emory's Fox Center for Humanistic Inquiry enabled the drafting of several sections of this book. Kimberly Jannarone read the manuscript at a key stage and offered generous and invaluable criticism. To these I offer my profound thanks.

Emory University
August 2012
N. W. S.

1

438 and All That

Sometime in the winter of 439/8 BC, the poet Euripides called upon the archon Glaucinus. Euripides was then in his 40s. His plays had competed at the Great or City Dionysia three or four times before,[1] beginning in the year 455, when his offering had included a play entitled *Daughters of Pelias*. Although four entries in seventeen years was not many, and his first victory had not come until 441,[2] Euripides certainly had some reputation to rely on as he sought to persuade Glaucinus, who as eponymous archon (the state official who gave his name to that civic year) was in charge of the forthcoming City Dionysia,[3] to grant him a slot at the competition.

We do not know how the archon made his selections. Euripides may simply have pitched his ideas for the four plays that would constitute his entry in the competition, or he may already have composed much of the verse and recited selections to the archon. Whatever the procedure, Glaucinus granted Euripides one of the three slots. Another competitor that year was his older rival, the poet Sophocles, who with the passing of Aeschylus some fifteen years before had become the dominant figure on the Attic stage. It is said that Sophocles never came in last in a competition, and when the festival took place in the spring of 438 he proved victorious once again, although we have lost the names of the plays with which he defeated Euripides.

At the City Dionysia each tragic poet offered four plays. Earlier in the century Aeschylus had competed with interconnected plays dramatizing different points in a longer mythic narrative, such as his *Oresteia*, *Lycourgeia*, or *Danaid* trilogies. Whether other playwrights followed suit is not clear, but by the 430s this practice had faded. When Euripides competed in the Theater of Dionysus on the south slope of the Acropolis on the 12th, 13th, or 14th of Elapheboleion (late March according to our calendar),[4] he did so with four unrelated plays: *Cretan Women*, *Alcmaeon in Psophis*, *Telephus*, and *Alcestis*.

We know next to nothing about the first two of these plays, but the third, *Telephus*, is perhaps the most famous lost play of Euripides,[5] known largely through the surviving parodies of it in the *Acharnians* and *Women at the Thesmophoria* by the comic playwright Aristophanes. Its story forms an earlier part of the larger narrative of the Trojan War. Telephus, a Greek who by marriage had become king of Mysia in the Troad and thus an ally of the Trojans, was wounded by Achilles in an early skirmish before the Greek expedition even sailed against Troy. Warned by an oracle that he could be healed only by the one who had wounded him, Telephus disguised himself as a beggar and entered the Greek camp. He was probably aided by Clytemnestra, wife of Agamemnon, leader of the Greek forces, and made a speech while still disguised to the assembled Greeks. When his disguise was penetrated, he seized Agamemnon's infant son Orestes, then took refuge on an altar, threatening to kill the child if Achilles would not help him. Whether Euripides actually staged this scene on the altar before the audience has been disputed, but the violence of the event certainly caused a sensation. The parodies in Aristophanes and the way the later visual tradition portrays this scene strongly favor the notion that Euripides staged the abduction and threatened murder of the baby Orestes rather than simply reporting these events by messenger speech. In any case, Telephus's forceful persuasion was successful, and Achilles healed his wound with part of the lance that had caused it. The play seems to have made a deep, though not necessarily favorable, impression on the public. This could well have been the first Dionysia attended by the young Aristophanes, who was perhaps as young as six and certainly no more than eight or nine at the time—but it clearly stuck in his mind and became the basis for brilliant parody more than a decade later. The scholarly editors of the Alexandrian age identified more lines parodied from the *Telephus* in Aristophanes' plays than from any other source—and its companion the *Alcestis* is his second most parodied play.

As we consider the effect of Euripides' plays of 438 on the public, it is worth noting that the *Telephus* as we reconstruct it is much more a story of thrilling adventures than painful moral dilemmas. A Greek ruling over a non-Greek population, Telephus must have had some questions about where his loyalties lay, and his speech seems to have questioned the Greeks' decision to go to war against Troy. Nonetheless in the end he agreed to guide the Greek expedition against his Trojan neighbors, affirming his ethnic Greek loyalties, and Achilles in return agreed to help heal him. It is unclear how an end to his shocking kidnapping and threat to the young Orestes was negotiated, but as in Euripides' later *Helen* or *Iphigenia in Tauris*, the ending was a happy one for the Greeks, as opposed to their barbarian adversaries.

We can infer one or two more very intriguing pieces of information about Euripides' entry in the play competition of 438 from one of the hypotheses, ancient scholarly notices about the play, preserved in some manuscripts. The hypothesis records the titles of the lost three companion plays, and in the absence of any other information, we may assume that the plays are listed in performance order, with the *Telephus* immediately preceding the *Alcestis*. The four plays each tragedian contributed to the City Dionysia normally consisted of three tragedies and a satyr play. Tragedies took their subject matter from the corpus of Greek myth. Satyr play drew on the world of myth as well, but its form was simultaneously both more constrained and freer. A satyr play's characters might be better- or lesser-known figures of myth, but its chorus was invariably composed of satyrs, hybrid human-animal figures who were followers and companions of Dionysus, god of wine and theater. The tragedians wove into their satyr plays well-known characters from myth such as Prometheus but were free to create new stories which involved those characters with the satyrs and their leader, Silenus. The satyr play, defined by its satyr chorus, always appeared fourth among the poet's offerings on the day of the festival. We know *Telephus* was not a satyr play, and nothing in the scant remnants of the others suggests they were either. The natural inference from the four titles reported in the production information of the hypothesis for the contest in 438 is that the *Alcestis* was the fourth play put on by Euripides that day—and yet it is certainly not a satyr play. Despite much speculation, no other play without a satyr chorus has ever been identified that *must* have filled the fourth slot in a tragedian's offering, so we cannot be sure whether this was an unrepeated experiment allowed by Glaucinus or part of a larger pattern. We can be sure, however, that the audience had not seen much like this before, a fact to which we shall return when we examine the play's themes below.

The plays themselves were only one part of the performances at the great spring festival in honor of Dionysus. The festival probably stretched over six days, with tragedians each offering a tetralogy on three successive days, five comic playwrights competing with one entry each on another day, and two days devoted to dithyramb, a choral form of poetry performed competitively by groups of men representing each of the ten Athenian tribes on one day, followed by ten boys' dithyrambs the next. The festival was designed not only to worship Dionysus with song and dance but also to celebrate the city of Athens itself before an audience drawn from the whole Greek world. By March the winter storms were ending, and the seas were navigable again, bringing merchants and visitors from around the Mediterranean world.

Athens in the 430s was a great imperial power and wished to be seen as such. Having led the successful efforts to defeat the Persian invasions of Greece in both 490 and 480/79, Athens had used her accumulated prestige and power to transform the anti-Persian defensive Delian League into an empire. By this period the celebration of the City Dionysia began with a procession into the orchestra of the theater which displayed the silver tribute contributed by the Athenians' allies to the Delian League, money which was even now helping to fund Pericles' great building program on the Acropolis, looming behind and above the citizens and visitors seated in the Theater of Dionysus on that March day. One display of material wealth followed another: after the tribute money came a parade of young Athenians, orphaned by war but now ready to serve their city. The citizens of Athens normally outfitted themselves for war when they were called up to serve as soldiers in defense of their empire. The orphan sons of those who fell in battle fighting for Athens, on attaining age eighteen that year, were given the armor and weaponry of a hoplite warrior by state, and at the Dionysia marched before their fellow citizens for the first time.[6] The wealth, power, and generosity of Athens were all on display in the theater before the festival's plays began.

Early in the afternoon therefore on the festival day allotted to Euripides, the actors and chorus of his *Telephus* left the stage and orchestra of the theater. A little later, one of the actors returned and began the performance of his *Alcestis*. What did the audience that day know about this play before it began? What frame of expectations did they have into which to fit—or not to fit—the experience that was about to unfold before them in the theater?

Some in the audience had doubtless attended a part of the festival called the Proagon a few days before, which offered a preview of things to come.[7] On that occasion, as was the custom for all the tragedians competing, Euripides had appeared in the Odeon of Pericles, a covered public hall next door to the theater, accompanied by his actors and choristers, suitably garlanded, to announce the *logoi* of his production.[8] This surely meant he announced the titles and perhaps, if the titles were insufficiently clear, the themes of his plays, but we do not know how much detail these *logoi* would have entailed. There is no evidence that the actors and chorus appeared in costume, nor could they have shown all the different costumes in any case, since both the actors and the choristers would play multiple roles in the course of performing four different plays. In short, it need not have been clear to the audience in the Odeon (far fewer than would attend the actual performances at the festival in any case) that the fourth play among Euripides' contributions to the forthcoming festival had no satyrs in it.

In the face-to-face society of Athens, it is unlikely that the lack of satyrs was a closely guarded secret. For one thing, it would not be possible to close rehearsals in an effective way for an open-air theater—though there is no certainty that the plays were rehearsed in the Theater of Dionysus itself.[9] Anyone who really wanted an advance glimpse of the offerings could probably get some idea. For the large majority of the audience, however, many of whom walked miles in from the Attic hinterland to attend the festival, there is no reason to assume they knew anything more about what to expect from *Alcestis* than what they could glean from its title.

External political events may have influenced the form of the *Alcestis* and its companion plays. C. W. Marshall has argued that Euripides may have chosen to expel the satyrs from his tetralogy partly in response to a decree passed by the assembly the year before in the archonship of Morychides (440/39) which forbade comic satire.[10] The question of whether or how the Athenians ever censored the freedom of the comic stage is vexed, but this decree is the most likely to be historical. Some politically prominent individuals did not like the way they were ridiculed in comedy. The intent of the decree was to eliminate direct attacks by name on individuals, but lacking a technical term for satire, the authors probably used for this purpose the phrase *mê kômôdein*, meaning "not to sing or perform a *kômos*." A *kômos* could be an abusive song aimed at individuals, but it was also the term for the rowdy groups that sang boisterous songs—and as such, could even apply to bands of satyrs. Marshall suggests that Euripides purposely (and subversively) misunderstood this phrase in the decree and used the *Alcestis* to show what banishing all "*kômos* behavior" from the Dionysiac festival would mean. Marshall further suggests that Euripides' startling innovation in turn prompted the comic poet Callias at the festival of 437 to produce a play called *Satyrs*, a theretofore unprecedented title for an Old Comedy, and that these satyrs may well have protested Euripides' decision to banish them from his play.

Marshall sees in the tetralogy of 438 a political protest based on free speech: Telephus in his play pleads for the right to speak freely, and the banished satyrs testify by their absence to the result of a ban on *kômôdein*. Whether one accepts these political allusions or not, it is quite plausible that the curious incident of satyrs who were not there in 438 produced a ripple effect. Moreover, Marshall makes a compelling case that nothing like the *Alcestis* had occupied the fourth slot in a tetralogy before, and there is no positive evidence that Euripides or any other tragedian ever offered a satyr-less fourth play at the City Dionysia.[11] The satyrs who were not there startled somebody.

That makes the collision of audience expectation, framed by years of watching satyr play as the conclusion to each tragic tetralogy, with the experience of the *Alcestis* as it unfolds on the stage uniquely interesting. There are many layers of meaning that can be discerned through careful and repeated study of a text, meanings that can be teased out by comparing an image here with a phrase there in an ever-widening web of intra- and intertextuality. That is not, however, the experience of an audience in the theater, especially an audience which has never seen this particular play before. The first-time audience must make sense of the linear experience of the play as it is performed. Moreover, the plays of the great tragedians were never re-performed at the City Dionysia in their lifetimes; the audience could never go back and attend that performance again.[12] To understand its original impact, we must re-imagine that first performance as it would have been experienced by an audience that had never seen or read the play—and might well not have known there were no satyrs in it.

The Myth(s)

The play's title, *Alcestis*, provided the audience with its first frame of reference. The myth of the king Admetus, whose wife Alcestis sacrificed her life for his, could have been familiar to many in the audience through songs and other oral sources not known to us today. In Homer there is only a brief reference to "the son of Pheres" (Admetus, at *Iliad* 2. 763), while there may have been a bit more in the lost *Catalogue of Women* by Hesiod.[13] The *Library* of mythology, compiled in the first or second century AD but attributed to the earlier Alexandrian scholar Apollodorus, talks about Admetus in two separate places: one story tells how the god Apollo was condemned by Zeus to serve the mortal king Admetus, and another relates the tale of Admetus' marriage to Alcestis.

Apollodorus' version of the marriage story contains elements much more complex than the events presupposed by Euripides' play. In Apollodorus, Alcestis' father sets a test for her suitors: they must yoke together a lion and a boar to pull a chariot before he will give up his daughter. Admetus accomplishes the task only with the help of Apollo but fails to offer sacrifice to the goddess Artemis at the wedding. Artemis fills the wedding chamber with snakes and apparently—though Apollodorus is not explicit here—condemns Admetus to an early death. Then Apollo obtains from the Fates the chance for Admetus to find a substitute, and "when his day to die came," Alcestis sacrifices herself. Apollodorus preserves two versions of the ending to this story: one in which Persephone, queen of the underworld, sends Alcestis back to the living, and another in which she is rescued by Heracles.[14]

It is possible then that the story of Apollo's enslavement to Admetus and that of Alcestis' sacrifice for her husband were originally separate myths; the version in which Persephone releases her may have had nothing to do with Apollo. Given the contradictions in these accounts, and their late attestation, it is not possible to say with certainty what details, especially of character motivation, a fifth-century Athenian audience would have had in mind. They need only have known that Alcestis died in the place of her husband Admetus—and somehow came back from the dead.

The story of Alcestis had, however, been staged in Athens at least once before Euripides' version. At least a generation earlier, the tragedian Phrynichus had produced an *Alcestis* at the Dionysia, and more than one scholar has guessed that it was a satyr play.[15] If so, audience members who remembered that performance or had heard of it might on the basis of the title expect that Euripides' current production would bring in a satyr chorus. Phrynichus' version was at least in the living memory of Euripides himself, for the Roman scholar Servius, commenting on Vergil's *Aeneid* many centuries later, asserts that Euripides borrowed from Phrynichus the motif of Death cutting Alcestis' hair with his sword.[16] On the other hand, Phrynichus won his first victory at the Dionysia before 508, and won again in 476, presumably near the end of his career.[17] Almost no one under the age of 50 in Euripides' audience could remember that last production. Phrynichus' otherwise undateable *Alcestis* might have been one of the very first plays that Euripides himself, born no earlier than 490, saw, but few others in 438 would have a clear memory.

Alcestis' name in the title alone thus would not have been enough to create a clear audience expectation of a tragedy rather than a satyr play, or vice versa. While male names (such as *Sisyphus*, *Lycurgus*, or *Cyclops*) or collectives (*Trackers*) dominate the lists of satyr play titles, as with tragedy at large, we do know that Aeschylus wrote a satyr play called *Amymone*, Sophocles a *Nausikaa*, Ion an *Omphale*. Moreover, we are told that Phrynichus was the first tragedian to introduce a female character onstage (*en têi skênêi*).[18] If one takes these words literally, this means he was the first to include a female role among the speaking characters onstage, as opposed to portrayals of a female chorus in the orchestra. It is very tempting to speculate that the *Alcestis*, his only known play named for an individual female character, wrought that particular revolution—all the more reason for such an innovative tragedy to be remembered forty years later.

The position of *Alcestis* on the program remains the chief and strongest argument for what the audience would expect when the play took the stage. All of the audience's past experience, man and boy, had taught them that a satyr play closed the day's performance. In the absence of any information to the contrary, the likeliest assumption is that most members of that audience in 438 expected Euripides' *Alcestis* to be a satyr play and only discovered as the performance unfolded that there were no satyrs to be found in it.

Production Conditions

The *Alcestis* was produced in the Theater of Dionysus on the south slope of the Acropolis in Athens. Nothing beyond a few stones remains of that fifth-century BC theater, and most elements of its reconstruction are controversial. The hillside formed the sloped audience space or cavea, with built seats at the front for magistrates, priests, and other officials, and probably wooden benches behind for the ordinary citizens. There is some evidence that citizens sat in wedged sections according to tribe, so that the theater mirrored the political organization of Athens. The seating capacity may have exceeded 15,000 (as it certainly did by the end of the next century), allowing a significant proportion of the adult male citizen population to see and hear the plays.[19] Non-citizens including foreign guests and probably some women sat at the back of the theater or on the sides.[20] In the middle was the orchestra or dancing place for the chorus. The chorus entered by one or both of the side entrances (called *parodoi*).

Behind the orchestra stood the *skênê* or scene building. Whether the fifth-century theater possessed a raised stage and, if so, how high that stage rose above the orchestra, has been long and not very fruitfully debated on archaeological grounds. Yet the relation of stage and orchestra as performance spaces is very important to our understanding of the play's whole effect. For the sound of individual actors' voices to carry in this large, open-air space it seems virtually certain that the actors needed a hard, reflective surface both behind them (the *skênê*) and beneath them (the stage). Our texts of tragedy show no certain example of chorus members entering the orchestra from the scene building or leaving the orchestra to enter within the scene building, so we might think of orchestra and stage as quite separate. Evidence from fifth-century comedy, however, which was performed in the same theater space, suggests that movement between the two spaces may have seemed possible. Presumably then the stage surface did not rise very high above the orchestra, and steps or some other access between the two levels must have been available. Some elevation of the stage, though, would have had great advantages for both sight lines and sound. Gods or mortals could appear on the roof of the scene building (as Athena likely did in Sophocles' *Ajax* a year or two before the *Alcestis*), and the crane or *mechanê*, a simple lever and fulcrum mechanism, could be used for mid-air appearances or flying (as Euripides' *Medea* demonstrated seven years after our play),[21] though the *Alcestis* requires none of this.

All performers in Greek tragedy were male, whatever the characters they portrayed. Both actors and choristers performed in masks that covered their entire heads (with a wig attached to the facial mask) as well as costumes. The use of masks enabled actors to play many parts within a given play. Aristotle tells us that in early tragedy there was only one actor, though he played multiple roles. Aeschylus then introduced a second actor and Sophocles a third. Although no ancient source tells us this explicitly, the limitation of the stage forces to three actors seems to be a regulation for fairness in competition (on which more in a moment). By the time Euripides premiered the *Alcestis*, three actors were available (and, to judge from its fragments, almost certainly employed by him in the *Telephus*). It is physically possible, however, for two actors to play the whole of the *Alcestis* (true also for the even later *Medea*). Silent characters did not count toward the three-actor limit, nor, it seems, did child performers (of whom more below). Thus the actors' parts in this play could have been divided between a leading actor (the Greek technical term is protagonist) and one assistant, perhaps as follows:

Protagonist: Apollo, Slave Woman, Alcestis, Child, Heracles, Pheres
Second Actor: Death, Admetus, Slave[22]

This looks imbalanced, with one actor carrying a very large share of the performance, and it seems much more practical to give to a third actor some of the roles here assigned to the protagonist, though proof is impossible.

More intriguing is the question of which roles the protagonist would choose to play. The overall competition at the Dionysia took place among the complete offerings by each playwright. A board of judges voted to award the prizes.[23] Technically, the prize went to the *choregos* or producer who financed the staging of those plays, though the later literary tradition always represents the poets themselves as the prizewinners. By 438 the city had established an additional prize for actors, but only the protagonists were allowed to compete for it. Although it is not until twenty years later that documentary proof survives to show that a man could win the acting contest while performing in a group of plays that did not win first place,[24] from the moment that an actors' contest exists, the actors must have been interested in playing the roles that would show them to best advantage in their own contest. Moreover, this "three-actor rule" constrained a poet writing for the Attic stage in how he structured his play. Under these conditions, the most natural way to compose a play is around the through-line of one leading character. "Leading character" does not necessarily mean "hero" or "heroine" in an evaluative sense: the structural center need not be the center of moral or even narrative interest.[25] It is nonetheless an interesting question whether Euripides built this play around the title character Alcestis or around her husband Admetus, who is onstage a much larger proportion of the time. Technical considerations enter in as well: the part of Alcestis is musically more demanding, given the lyrics she sings as she enters, and so a protagonist competing for the prize would probably consider hers the more bravura of the two roles.

The question of which roles were performed by the same actor is of more than antiquarian interest as we consider how an audience experiences the play in performance. While masks would completely conceal the facial identity of the actor, the audience may have been subliminally aware of vocal identity.[26] We have no evidence that actors altered their voices significantly to portray different characters, perhaps not even to differentiate male and female voice,[27] and the demands of vocal projection in the vast open-air space of the Theater of Dionysus would have significantly limited their ability to do so. Thus the slave woman who tells the audience what Alcestis does within the house and even quotes her verbatim could have been speaking in recognizably the same voice as Alcestis herself when she appears. These groupings of voices have the potential to add layers of meaning and associations to those present on the surface of the text, subtly underscoring sympathies and antipathies.

The ancient Greek experience of plays differed sharply from ours. Masked performers in a huge open-air space sang and spoke in verse, and the chorus of fifteen singers also added dance to the mix. While drawing on a familiar body of myth, the poets conceived each play as a single, unique staging of the story—no one could come back the next day to see the play again or catch anything they missed at the first and only performance. With this framework in mind, our pre-performance preparations are now complete; it is time for the players to take the stage.

2

The Action of the Play

Greek tragedy is woven from the interaction of actors onstage and a chorus (composed of 15 members in Euripides' time) in the orchestra. All of their utterances are in verse, though recitative (chanted) meters predominate in the actors' performances while more musically complex and lyrical forms underlie the choral contributions. In a sense, actors and chorus even speak different languages (as different, say, as Mexican and peninsular Spanish): the odes of the chorus are in the Doric dialect (not native to Athens), while the actors employ Attic Greek. These aural differences, along with the physical entrances and exits of actors and chorus, articulate the whole of the drama.

Prologue

The word "prologue" today often means the preliminary part of any story. In Greek drama it has a more technical meaning: the prologue is everything that occurs before the entrance of the chorus. While the characters who appear in the prologue often give background information useful for understanding the story about to be enacted, it is important to remember that this is not its sole, nor even necessarily its primary, purpose. The prologue functions as an induction, drawing the audience imaginatively into the world of the play.

The *Alcestis* begins with the god Apollo emerging from the central door in the scene building (*skênê*),[1] which he immediately labels the house of Admetus. He carries a bow (as we learn from line 39) and presumably is costumed in a way that will help identify him visually.[2] In a brief speech he outlines how he was sentenced by Zeus to serve a mortal, was treated well by Admetus, the ruler of Pherae in Thessaly, and therefore became his protector, even to the extent of "tricking" the Fates (line 11) into allowing Admetus to escape his own death by finding a substitute to die in his place.[3] Though others refused him, his wife Alcestis chose to sacrifice herself. Now is the fated day, and Apollo must leave a house about to be polluted by death. As he does so, he spots Death approaching.

What does Death look like, and how does his appearance shape audience reaction to him? While many gods appeared on the Athenian stage, personified abstractions such as Death (Thanatos) are rare. Death appears in the company of his brother Sleep (Hypnos) in the text of Homer and then in painted scenes on pottery of the fifth century, but his only other known appearance on the Athenian stage was in Phrynichus' *Alcestis*. On vases from the second half of the fifth century he is usually an older, bearded figure with wings.[4] In her delirium Alcestis later sees a winged underworld figure coming for her (line 262, *pterôtos Haidas*), so it is probably safe to assume that Death is so costumed here.[5] He seems to handle the dead gently in the visual arts, though a still-living woman attempts to flee from him on a white ground lekythos painted in Athens not many years distant from our play.[6] Any judgement on the emotional impact of Death's appearance here will necessarily be speculative,[7] but the little evidence to survive suggests he is indeed a figure of antipathy.

Death also carries a sword, and the visual confrontation of two armed figures, Apollo with his bow defending the house and Death attacking, paradoxically hints at the physical violence which is never represented on the tragic stage. Instead, a less-than-dignified wrangle of words ensues. Death's first words resound in a more excited meter as he blames Apollo for cheating him of Admetus and suspects, rightly, that Apollo is trying to prevent him from taking Alcestis. Apollo's attempts to bribe Death with the promise of richer grave offerings for a postponement of fate are fruitless. Apollo departs, prophesying obscurely that "one will come to the house of Pheres from Eurystheus" (lines 65–6) and take away from Death by force what he has refused here to give as a favor. Audience members familiar with the myth may recognize who the one sent from Eurystheus is, but Apollo does not name him. Death then enters the palace. His sword, otherwise unusual for Death but borrowed from Phrynichus' portrayal, casts him as a priest about to cut a lock of Alcestis' hair, making her his destined sacrifice (line 74).

Parôdos

The stage is thus left empty for the arrival of the chorus into the orchestra. The tone of the preceding 78 lines is hard to assess, but if the original audience had been expecting a satyr drama, including its typical play with traditional mythology, the aggressive encounter between two divinities just witnessed would not seem out of place. Only as a chorus of old men, rather than one composed of satyrs, enters slowly into the orchestra does it become clear that this is no satyr play but apparently a fourth tragedy for the day.

A marginal note (scholion) in a manuscript tells us that the chorus is composed of old men and, unusually, divided into two half-choruses in this entrance song. Surviving manuscripts are centuries later than the original performances, and we have no reason to assume that the poets themselves wrote "stage directions." The age of the chorus here may be only an ancient scholar's inference from line 212, where the servant refers to them as old friends of the royal house. They are certainly citizens of Pherae. One of the ancient hypotheses or prefatory notices to the play also suggests that there are five individual voices singled out among the chorus.[8] If the original performance did use two half-choruses, the members probably appeared from both side entrances (the *parodoi*) and mingled together in the orchestra.

Their first verses are delivered in a marching meter called anapaests (lines 77–85), as the chorus members assemble, followed by two further sections of verse, more complex but metrically identical to each other. Much of the choral verse in Greek tragedy is in such strophic pairs. We believe that the choristers danced as they sang these sections, first in one direction or dance figure during the strophe, then in a mirror or reverse figure during the antistrophe which returned them to their original position.

If the audience is uncertain how to interpret the appearance of these milling choristers who are not satyrs, the chorus itself is unsure what to make of the external signs of the palace of Admetus. They know this is the fated day for Alcestis' death, but they scan the scene anxiously for ritual indications of mourning and question each other whether she has indeed died. They end on notes of despair, concluding that appeals for aid to far-off prophetic shrines of Apollo or Zeus Ammon would not avail. They mention Aesclepius, the son of Apollo, as one who could have raised Alcestis from the dead—but Zeus struck him down, and now there is no one with such power.

Episode

The chorus sees a female slave emerging from the palace and immediately asks her whether the queen is alive or dead. Her reply is one of the most famous—and sophistically riddling—lines in the play (141): "You could say she is both alive and dead." The chorus is puzzled, but the servant explains that her fate is coming inexorably and so she lies on the very verge between life and death.

In response to the chorus' praise of Alcestis as "the best woman/wife beneath the blessed sun," the servant affirms it by relating the final preparations for death she is making within the house. She has bathed herself (something mourners would normally do for her body after death), prayed to the goddess of the hearth, Hestia, for her children, and bidden farewell to the altars and finally her marriage bed in a powerful speech which the servant quotes directly (177–82):

> O marriage bed, where I lost my youthful
> maidenhood to this husband, for whom I now die,
> farewell. I do not hate you, but you alone have destroyed
> me. Dreading to betray (*prodounai*) you and my spouse
> I die. Some other woman will possess you,
> no more virtuous, but perhaps more fortunate.

This is the first instance of the language of "betrayal" in the play; Alcestis sees her sacrifice as death in defense of the bond her marriage bed embodies.[9] Farewells to her children and servants follow. Only when prompted by the chorus does the servant report on her husband Admetus. He weeps, holding her and begging her in turn not to "betray" herself (again *prodounai*, 202) by dying[10]—an impossible request. The servant then goes back in to report the arrival of the chorus, leaving them alone in the theater.

First Stasimon

A short ode from the chorus follows. The strophe (213–25) calls first on Zeus, then on Apollo the Healer, to find a way out for Admetus (line 221). The antistrophe (226–37) grieves for his loss, calling on the whole land to mourn for this best of women. The last word of both sections is "Hades," signifying both the ruler of the underworld and his underworld kingdom itself. The old men close with generalizing verses asserting that marriage brings more pain than happiness. Bereft of his wife, the king will now lead a life that is no life at all.

Episode

Alcestis, Admetus, their children and servants emerge from the palace. Alcestis sings in a complex and emotional meter, while her husband at first answers her in iambic trimeter, the meter of ordinary speech in Greek drama. Her first words invoke the light of the sun and the clouds in the sky. The convention of Greek drama was that all the action took place outdoors. Scenes that by the logic of the narrative should take place indoors could be staged with the use of the *eccyclêma*, a rolling platform that could be brought out through a doorway in the scene building with actors and even furniture placed on it. Some scholars presume that the *eccyclêma* was used here for Alcestis' entrance, but given the direct references to the light of the sun, it seems more likely that Alcestis emerges from the palace during the chorus' final verses, supported by one or more of those around her, and then sinks onto a couch placed for her by the servants.[11] She is hallucinating, seeing the infernal ferryman Charon and winged Hades himself leading her away,[12] and bids farewell to her children again.

After this lyric outburst, Alcestis speaks in much calmer trimeters as she reminds Admetus what he owes her. We learn that his father and mother refused to die in his place, but only she was willing to make this sacrifice. She asks that in return that Admetus not remarry (305), even though in the servant's earlier report of her farewell to her marriage bed (181–2), she has explicitly imagined another woman taking her place there.[13] Her motive, she explains, is to protect her children from a stepmother. She grieves over her children again, especially her daughter, growing up without a mother, and concludes thus (323–5):

> Farewell and be happy; and you, husband,
> may boast you married the best (*aristê*) wife,
> and you, children, were born of the best mother.

This is not a comfortable speech for modern sensibilities. A century ago the great Greek scholar Gilbert Murray translated these verses with an eye toward performance thus:

> Farewell. God keep you happy.—Husband dear,
> Remember that I failed thee not; and you,
> My children, that your mother loved you true.

Even though his was a rhyming translation and he may have needed "dear" to make a partial rhyme with "were" in the preceding line, Murray was apparently unwilling to present Alcestis as a woman whose proffered comfort to her husband and children was that they should thereafter speak of her as the "best" or "noblest wife" and "best mother." The adjective *aristê* here is precisely the same one both the chorus and the servant use to praise her earlier (151–2). Alcestis knows that what she has given her husband is far more than he could ever repay, and she expects this to be acknowledged.

Before Admetus can even speak, the chorus reassures her that he will do as she asks, unless he is out of his mind. Admetus affirms this, promising never to remarry. He hates his parents for their unwillingness to sacrifice themselves for him. In a significant catchphrase from sophistic thought, he declares that they were family (339) "in word but not in deed." Instead he will honor Alcestis by declaring perpetual mourning in his house, with no music or revelry. He promises to have her likeness (*demas*) made by craftsmen to lie in bed with him as he mourns, while he will lie with her in the tomb when he dies.

Alcestis calls on her children to witness their father's promises and formally hands them over to him (371–8):

> Alc. Children, you yourselves have heard your father
> saying that he will never marry another wife
> to your disadvantage nor dishonor me.
> Adm. I say it now, and I will fulfill it.
> Alc. On these conditions, receive the children from my hand.
> Adm. I receive them, a dear gift from a dear hand.
> Alc. Become now a mother to these children in place of me.
> Adm. It is most necessary for me, since they are bereft of you.

As the darkness overwhelms her, she speaks once more to her children, then dies.

This onstage death is remarkable and perhaps unique. Many perish by violence in Greek tragedy, but their deaths regularly take place offstage and are reported by messengers. Only the death of Hippolytus in Euripides' play of the same name seems at all comparable. Even there the violent cause of death, the crash of Hippolytus' chariot as the result of his father Theseus' curse, occurs offstage.[14] The dying Hippolytus is brought back onstage for his final exchange with Theseus, and it may moreover be open to interpretation as to whether he dies immediately after his final request that they cover his face (*Hipp.* 1458), just moments before he is carried within the palace, and the play ends. Alcestis alone then dies without violence in full view of the audience, which must have made a powerful emotional impact.

Our text records a moving lament sung by her son over Alcestis' body, proclaiming that, with her death, the house is destroyed. Other children appear in Greek tragedy, but the closest parallel for this scene is from a later play of Euripides, the *Andromache* (505ff.), where a child sings a few lines of lament in duet with his mother. The scene in *Alcestis* is much fuller; presumably boys, appropriately masked and costumed, played both the (silent) daughter and son here. Given the musical complexity and length of the son's lament, A. M. Dale thought that the actor who has played Alcestis could sing these verses while the child actor mimes the action over the body, but G. M. Sifakis thought there would have been boys with the musical training to carry off such a solo.[15] If Sifakis is right, the novel effect of the boy's voice must only have increased the powerful emotional impact of the visual tableau here, with son, daughter, and husband all gathered around the body.

Admetus instructs the chorus to remain and sing a paean "to the god below," proclaims a year's mourning, and accompanies his children and his wife's body into the palace, leaving the stage empty again.

Second Stasimon

The chorus' ode says farewell to Alcestis and bids Hades and Charon the ferryman know that they are carrying by far the best woman of all (*gunaik' aristan*) away to the underworld. They promise that her praises will be sung both at the Carneian festival of Apollo in Sparta and in Athens, implying renown across the whole Greek world.[16] They wish, but know they wish in vain, to fetch her back from Hades. They proclaim their hatred for any woman Admetus might marry after her, reflect adversely on his parents' refusal to save him, and wish that they might be fortunate enough to marry wives as loving as Alcestis.

Episode

A new character appear onstage from a side entrance, recognizable by the lion skin he wears (and perhaps the club he carries) as the great hero Heracles. The chorus certainly has no need to ask his identity but, after assuring him Admetus is at home, enquires after his mission. Heracles replies that he has been sent by Eurystheus to capture the horses of Diomedes: Eurystheus' name may remind some in the audience of Apollo's promise (lines 65–9) of the coming of such a hero. The chorus seems to enjoy telling him that the horses of his future host, Diomedes, are man-eaters (484ff.), but this does not faze Heracles.

Admetus re-emerges from the house to greet his guest. Heracles recognizes by Admetus' shorn hair (*kourâi penthimôi*, 512) and other signs that he is in mourning. Greek theater masks included the attached hair or wig. Admetus should not have appeared in the first scene with shorn hair, since Alcestis is not yet dead. The actor thus may have exchanged his first mask for a new one with shorn hair for this scene. Characters' lines in Greek drama can refer to changes of facial expression that are not possible with a mask and must therefore be left to the audience's imagination. By analogy the cut hair might also be left to imagination, but since a second mask with short hair was well within the technical capabilities of the theater at this period, it seems likelier that this significant change in Admetus' appearance was really represented to the audience.

With immediate concern Heracles asks after Admetus' children, his father—and then his wife, Alcestis. While Admetus briefly assures him that his children and father are well, he says riddlingly of his wife (521; compare the servant at 141), "She is alive and yet not alive—and it grieves me." Responding to Heracles' further bewildered questions, he asserts that, once Alcestis chose to die for him, she was already as good as dead. Though Heracles demurs, Admetus seems to change the subject and says that the woman who has died was closely tied to his house but not related, playing sophistically on Greek notions of just what kind of a relationship marriage was. Heracles still does not want to stay in a house of mourning, but Admetus presses him with the offer of rooms away from the rest of the house. Agreeing, Heracles exits with a servant.

The chorus is astonished, questioning whether Admetus is a "fool" (*môros*, 552) for welcoming a guest when all are in mourning. Admetus insists he owes hospitality to Heracles and defends deceiving his friend on the grounds that Heracles would not have stayed, had he known the truth. His departing statement is that his house (566–7) "does not know how to reject or dishonor guests."

Third Stasimon

The tone of the performance shifts significantly as the chorus, retreating from their outburst at Admetus, sings the praises of this repeatedly hospitable (*poluxeinos*, 568) house that once received Apollo as its guest, when he endured the shepherd's life in service to Admetus.[17] Their change of language and meter carries the audience away to a pastoral vision of Apollo piping to a military troop of lions (*ila*, 581), while lynxes and fawns dance together in the fields to the music of his lyre.[18] Apollo blesses Admetus' kingdom with fertility, and the chorus concludes its praise of Admetus' actions thus (600–5):

> Good breeding
> shows itself in respect to *aidôs*.
> All of wisdom dwells in honorable men. I am in awe.[19]
> Courage abides in my soul
> that this god-fearing man will accomplish dear things.

For all its apparent simplicity, the Greek here is not easy to render. The chorus invokes *aidôs* (respect for self and others, a sense of shame) as a standard, but it is something other than wisdom and honor, to which they turn. Excellent translators sometimes relegate the "god-fearing man" to a prepositional phrase in their translations, and thereby make him the recipient of action, rather than the agent.[20] Nothing, however, should obscure the first sign of meaningful hope from this oft-despairing chorus: its prediction that Admetus will accomplish "dear things" (*kedna*) is not to be dismissed lightly.[21]

Episode

Admetus emerges from the palace again with the body of Alcestis and her funeral cortege. He invites the chorus to speak their farewells, but they have already spotted his father Pheres approaching.

Pheres proclaims his sympathy for his son, praises Alcestis, and offers funeral gifts for her. His statement that such marriages as his son's are "profitable for men; otherwise it's not worth marrying" (627–8) is certainly not well calculated for his audience, and Admetus responds with fury: his father, who refused to help him when he was in danger of dying, is not welcome at the funeral. He is a coward who cannot really be Admetus' father. In fact, his deceased wife is his true family and his real father and mother; he is now dead to his father and will give the care a child owes to his parents to Alcestis.

The chorus begs him to stop, but neither he nor Pheres takes any notice. Pheres denies any obligation to his son, asserts that life is just as sweet to the old as to the young, and accuses his son in turn of cowardice. He taunts Admetus by suggesting he prolong his life yet further by marrying a series of wives to die for him. Amidst mutual accusations of shamelessness (lack of *aidôs*, 727–8), Pheres departs, threatening his son with vengeance from Alcestis' brother, Acastus. Admetus orders the attendants to take up the body, and the funeral cortege departs, followed by the chorus, leaving both stage and orchestra vacant.[22]

The departure of the chorus during the course of a play is quite unusual in Greek tragedy. Before Euripides, there is evidence for such a mid-play departure only in Aeschylus' *Eumenides* and in Sophocles' *Ajax*. In both these plays a well-heralded change of scene accompanies the chorus' exit and re-entrance: in Aeschylus, Orestes flees from Delphi to Athens, while Ajax in Sophocles leaves his tent and goes down to the beach to commit suicide. A quarter-century after the performance of *Alcestis*, Euripides would send away the chorus of his *Helen* so that Menelaus could arrive upon the scene completely unobserved. That chorus does then return to the same spot. It is worth pondering, however, whether the audience for the original production of *Alcestis* might have expected the action to shift from the palace to her tomb—or what other expectations they might have had after the remarkable tonal shifts of the preceding action.

What they receive is a new arrival from within the palace, a slave deeply distressed by the drunken and riotous behavior of his master's guest, Heracles. As he succinctly puts it, there are "two different songs to hear" (760), the mourning cries of his fellow servants and the drunken party songs of "some wretched robber and brigand" (766) whom his master insists on entertaining.

Heracles soon follows him out, abusing him for his sullen looks and service, and recommending drinking as a way to take the mind off sorrows. He insists that life cannot be so bad if the woman who died was not really related to the family. This the servant cannot bear, and he reveals the truth. Appalled by his own behavior, Heracles asks where the burial is taking place. Having informed him, the servant departs.

Left alone on stage, Heracles resolves to go and rescue Alcestis from Death, either by wrestling him at the tomb or, if he misses him there, by pursuing her to the underworld. As the audience will certainly know, just such a trip to Hades will be one of Heracles' most famous labors hereafter, bringing back the triple-headed guard dog of the underworld, Cerberus. In light of Admetus' nobility and hospitable nature, Heracles resolves to show himself no less noble and departs to the rescue.

Presumably Heracles leaves by the same side entrance through which Admetus and the funeral cortege departed. If the audience is not to imagine them colliding into each other on the road, the stage and orchestra must again be empty for an appreciable time. Only after a suitable pause can Admetus and his followers return via that same side entrance.

Kommos

The succeeding hundred lines, led off by Admetus but with the chorus joining in, form a lyrical lament or *kommos* for Alcestis. The bitterness of his loss leads Admetus to wish he had never married, and he reproaches the chorus who prevented him from hurling himself into the grave with this "best of wives" (again *aristês*, 899). As comfort, the old men of the chorus can merely offer the example of one in their family who lost an only son, yet somehow bore his grief.

Admetus asks how he can ever enter his house again as he remembers coming to this door before, bringing his wife home in the marriage procession. The scene on the stage is like a photographic negative of that past occasion, structurally the same but with all the values reversed. As Admetus notes, then as he led his wife by the hand (917), the throng of revelers (*kômos*, 918) sang marriage songs, now they sing laments (*goos*, 922); then they all wore wedding white, now black; then they went to the marriage bed, now to his empty widower's couch. Admetus realizes that he will be able to endure neither living in his empty house, robbed of his wife's presence, nor public encounters outside his house where young women will remind him of his wife and his enemies will revile him for his cowardice.

Fourth Stasimon

The lyric form shifts from lament as the chorus sings an ode to Necessity. No altars and no prayers move this goddess, who has caught Admetus in her coils. The chorus urges Admetus to honor Alcestis' burial place not simply as the tomb of a mortal, but as the gods themselves are honored, an object of reverent awe (*sebas*, 998). In language reminiscent of Homeric heroes,[23] the chorus itself even performs the invocation of her blessing that it anticipates passing travelers will offer:

> "This woman who once died for her husband
> is now a blessed spirit (*makaira daimon*).
> Hail, o lady, and may you grant us favor."
> Such words will supplicate her.
>
> (1002–5)

Episode and Exodos

Heracles returns, leading a veiled woman,[24] and immediately reproaches Admetus for not telling him of his wife's death. He tells his host that he is departing at once for his assigned task to capture the horses of Diomedes, but he asks to leave behind with Admetus the woman he has just won, he says, in a public athletic contest. Admetus apologizes for his deception, then begs Heracles at length not to ask this favor of him, since having this woman in the house will only remind him of his lost wife and increase his misery. Heracles offers conventional words of comfort, but when he suggests his friend will marry again to end his grief, Admetus violently rejects the notion. Heracles returns to the woman at hand and appeals to Admetus' noble nature (*gennaios*, 1097) to take her in. Admetus still refuses—unless, he says, Heracles will be angry with him. He then yields—but demurs again, when Heracles insists that Admetus not entrust the woman to servants but take her from his own hand. More than a hundred lines after the veiled woman first appeared, Admetus reaches out to take her with his right hand (*cheiri dexiâi*, 1115, a gesture deeply evocative of marriage).[25] He does so "as if I were cutting off the Gorgon's head" (1118)—and discovers that the woman is his wife, Alcestis.

Admetus fears she is a phantom (*phasma*, 1127), a conjecture by no means irrational in the world of tragedy (where actors playing ghosts could appear).[26] Heracles, however, reassures him that she is real, explaining he fought with Death for her. Only after several exchanges of joy and explanation between the two men does Admetus ask why his wife does not speak. Heracles explains that until the third day after she is purified from her consecration to the dead, it is not right for him to hear her speak (1144–5).[27] He bids his friend to continue to be both just and pious toward guests and takes his leave, despite Admetus' pleas for him to stay.

Admetus decrees that choruses and sacrifices should be performed in honor of these happy events and acknowledges his good fortune. The chorus sings five closing lines about the gods bringing unexpected things to pass, lines which also appear in our manuscripts at the end of several other Euripides plays,[28] and departs.

3

Themes of the Play

On the score of beautiful morality there is none of the pieces of Euripides so deserving of praise as Alcestis …
                    August Wilhelm von Schlegel

When Schlegel spoke these words in his famous lectures on drama in Vienna in 1808, he was echoing the tradition of two millenia, which idealized Alcestis as the perfectly self-sacrificing wife and mother.[1] This is the Alcestis of eighteenth- and nineteenth-century painting, bathed in the radiant light of her selflessness, surrounded by her fainting family.[2] Much has changed in the last two centuries, not only in predominant Western views of marital duty, devotion, and the roles of husband and wife, but also in expectations of what this particular play might have to say on these subjects. For readers and viewers down to the early nineteenth century, the classification of the *Alcestis* as a tragedy was no more in question than that of Sophocles' *Œdipus*. With the publication in 1834 of Dindorf's edition of *Alcestis*, including the second hypothesis, it became generally known that the play occupied the fourth position in Euripides' tetralogy and therefore stood in for a satyr play; the genre of the play and its seriousness were suddenly open to question.

Yet genre alone cannot completely determine meaning or even tone. In the last century the tragic seriousness of much else in Euripides has come to seem more problematic for scholars, students, and even the fortunate few who have seen his plays performed. To contemporary audiences Euripides seems to delight in testing boundaries and confounding categories, and his first surviving play offers ample proof of these tendencies.

The House and the Door

"O house of Admetus" are Apollo's first words as he emerges from its door, and the physical presence of the palace dominates the action of the play just as much as does the House of Atreus in Aeschylus' *Agamemnon* or the House of Cadmus in the *Bacchae*. It pervades the language of the play as well, as more than eighty instances of terms for house (*domos*), home (both *oikos* and *dôma*), and halls (*melathra*) are scattered throughout the play.[3] For Admetus the house is virtually animate, possessed of knowledge and volition: he defends his decision to conceal the truth from Heracles by saying "My halls do not know how to reject or dishonor guests" (566–7). This statement prompts the chorus' most lyrical stasimon, the third, which begins by invoking "O always hospitable house of a free man" (568–9).[4]

The audience knows more of the unseen interior of this house, both at present and in an imagined future, than perhaps any other house in Greek tragedy. The female servant's speech to the chorus takes us on a virtual tour of the interior as Alcestis bids farewell to its altars, the servants, her children, and finally her marriage bed (152–98). When Admetus and the chorus return from the graveside, his first despairing lines lament "the hateful sights of empty halls" (861–2). When he cries out "O figure of my house (*o schêma domôn*), how shall I enter in, how shall I dwell there …?" (912–13), the familiar form (*schêma*) evokes only its emptiness and loss.[5] His imagination then tours again the neglected and slowly decaying interior of the house bereft of its mistress and the children and servants bewailing her loss (941–9).

The boundaries and defenses of this house loom large. Apollo attempts to defend it with words against invading Death but fails. Admetus is more successful in driving from its doors its former master, his father (even Apollo once calls it "the house of Pheres"

[65]), who is no longer welcome there. The parallelism in performance seems plain; Anne Burnett suggests, linking the two scenes:

> Since Heracles is young … and a bringer of life, while Pheres is old and mean and associated with death, the king [Admetus] has shown himself truly king by driving out old Hunger and bringing in Wealth and Health.[6]

Yet the house that Admetus defends against Pheres is already broken. It requires Heracles' further action to restore the meaning of the house, and he does so as Admetus hesitates at its boundary, unwilling to face life either inside the house or outside without Alcestis (941–61).

The house defines itself by inclusion and exclusion, and the door is a key marker in the process. In his first exchanges with Heracles, Admetus says that the woman who has died was a stranger (*othneios*, 532) and not a blood relation (*suggenês*), though necessarily connected (*anagkaia*, 533) and therefore related in another way. Heracles therefore concludes that this death is an external grief, literally a "suffering from outside the door" (*thuraiou pêmatos*, 778), as he terms it in his exchanges with the servant later.[7] A wife, because she comes from the outside, is always technically *thuraios*, but Heracles cannot think of Alcestis that way.

As in English, so in Greek the notion of "house" is invested with a meaning far more than physical. While Alcestis nowhere gives a simple statement of the reasons for her choice to die in the place of Admetus, houses and control of the house play a large part in her imagination and explanation of her actions. Her second utterance onstage calls out in farewell to "Earth and roofed halls and bridal chambers of my Iolcian homeland" (248–9),[8] and she explicitly notes that she could have let Admetus die, remarried a local lord, and "dwelt in a house rich with royal wealth" (286).[9] Moreover, the promise she asks of Admetus not to remarry is grounded explicitly in her desire that their son and daughter become "rulers of my house" (*despotas emôn domôn*, 304)—note the singular possessive adjective. It is arguable then that Alcestis dies to preserve the house, which will remain hers as long as no other wife supplants her.

Yet, of course, in saving the house she destroys it. In this she differs from such later Euripidean women as Macaria in the *Children of Heracles* or Iphigenia in the *Iphigenia at Aulis*, who offer to sacrifice themselves for the city or the host of armies assembled for war. Perhaps the *polis* can be saved by such a sacrifice, but the *oikos* is laid waste. Even as she is dying, Admetus promises not just to remain an unmarried widower but to make the music and revelry which in the past filled "my house" (*emous domous*, 344) fall silent; he himself will never sing or play again, only mourn. He only envisions other aspects of the ruination of their house later, on his return from the funeral (861), but their son, lamenting over Alcestis' body, immediately sums up the reality: "With you gone, mother, our house is destroyed" (*olôlen oikos*, 414–15).

It therefore seems all the more significant that when Admetus, finally yielding to Heracles, says in three successive speeches that the veiled woman may be taken "into the house" (*domois*, 1110; *domous*, 1112; *dôma*, 1114), Heracles insists that he, not the house, must take her with his own hand.[10] It seems that the house cannot simply be restored by putting Alcestis back into it. Something else, which the house may symbolize but cannot fully embody, must be restored as well.

Husband and Wife

Royal marriages rarely turn out well in Greek tragedy. Wives kill their husbands intentionally (Clytemnestra in Aeschylus' *Agamemnon*) or inadvertently (Deinaira in Sophocles' *Trachinian Women*), husbands attempt to kill their wives (Menelaus in Euripides' *Helen*, Tereus in Sophocles' lost *Tereus*), and wives kill themselves rather than face their husbands (Jocasta in Sophocles' *Œdipus*, Phaedra in Euripides' *Hippolytus*)—to say nothing of parents who kill their children or vice versa. Indeed, some political and anthropological approaches to Greek tragedy suggest that death and destruction in the royal household, followed by lamentation and mourning in the society, form in Greek tragedy an underlying pattern of powerful social meaning for the constitution of the contemporary democratic society that staged the tragedies.[11] Yet for all the loss and mourning in between, the *Alcestis* begins and ends with the royal pair married to each other, and songs of joy for her restoration supplant the memorial choruses of lamentation promised to honor the queen's self-sacrifice.

The play is almost as reticent about their lives as husband and wife before this fateful day as it is about events hereafter. Euripides has structured the play in a way that suppresses large elements of the myth and obscures key preceding moments and choices that would otherwise flesh out their marital roles. Other sources tell us how Admetus, who in his youth had sailed with Jason on the Argo, won the hand of Alcestis from her father Pelias. These stories have familiar folktale elements. When Pelias challenges his daughter's suitors to a seemingly impossible task (yoke a lion and a boar together to draw a chariot), he could be any father unwilling to part with his daughter. Like many another hero, Admetus needs help to succeed, and his kind treatment of Apollo in the past explains the god's intervention here. The wrath of Artemis against the bridegroom could be an entirely separate story: when Admetus then failed to sacrifice to Artemis at his wedding, she sent snakes to fill the wedding chamber.[12] Yet there is no necessary connection between this story and the revelation that Admetus is fated to die young—but can be saved by Apollo's interference. In some versions of the myth, Alcestis is faced with her choice on her wedding night—and may even die immediately in her husband's stead. No trace of these elements can be found in Euripides' version. The play tells of no past heroic deeds by Admetus, even in the winning of his bride. Alcestis is already the mother of two children, but nothing in this play reveals precisely when Apollo won the favor for Admetus from the Fates and therefore when Alcestis made her choice to die. Instead, the play begins on her last day and only looks forward, never back.

At the same time, the categories of husband and wife are severely tested by the action. The promise Alcestis demands of her husband will effectively redefine Admetus in two ways. His promise not to remarry requires that he never again be a husband, only a widower, and his promise to be a mother as well as father to their children at the very least makes his own gender identity more fluid (377; see also below). In the midst of Admetus' angry confrontation with Pheres, he declares that Pheres and "that woman you live with" (734) are no longer his father and mother; instead, he will regard himself as the child of Alcestis (see further below).

Several scholars have suggested ways in which Alcestis' death seems to feminize Admetus.[13] They point to his fear that public opprobrium will confine him to the house, the inner space of a Greek household normally appropriate to women, there to spend his life in weeping and mourning, quintessentially female activities.[14] By cutting himself off from his parents (see below), Admetus isolates himself just as a new bride is cut off from her birth home, and in his powerful aversion against accepting the veiled woman, he exhibits the cultural norm of the reluctant bride rather than the eager groom.[15] Yet the confusion may be even deeper. When he returns from the burial, Admetus feels himself desperately out of place either indoors or out; he shrinks both from going out in public, where others will point to him as the man who allowed his wife to die in his place (954ff.), and from re-entering the palace whose empty and soon-to-be-disordered interior spaces will only remind him of the absence of his deceased wife (944ff.). His speech hints at confusion over his age identity as well, for he does not wish to associate at public festivals with young women who will remind him of his wife (952–3). He imagines an unidentified enemy publicly posing this question about him (957): "does he then seem to be a man (*anêr*)?"

The result of Alcestis' sacrifice seems then to endanger both Admetus' gender identity and status as an adult. The spatial dynamics of the play underscore these categorical confusions. Alcestis is the only woman in Greek tragedy to die onstage, and that death does more than defy general stage conventions about death or violence. Space is gendered in Greek drama, with interior, domestic space normally categorized as female, and outdoor, public space as male. Women who kill themselves in Greek tragedy do so in the privacy of the home, but Alcestis' sacrifice occurs in the open light of day, in full view of the citizen chorus as well as the audience.[16]

The restoration of both Admetus and Alcestis to their roles as husband and wife is facilitated by the performative ambiguity of the procession of actors and chorus returning from the graveside, as well as the insistence of Heracles. When Admetus compares the returning cortege of mourners to his memories of their original wedding, he activates a connection deeply felt in Greek culture. Artemidorus, whose second-century AD book on dream interpretation gives us so much insight into the symbolic imagination of the Greeks, more than once underscores the connection. "Both marriage and death have the same *logos*," he asserts, "because the attendant circumstances for both are similar." Elsewhere he explains: "the same things befall both a man marrying and a man dying, such as a procession of friends, both men and women, and garlands and spices and ointments."[17]

What converts the mourning procession into a remarriage celebration is Heracles' insistence on physically joining the hands of Admetus and the veiled woman. The scene leading up to this moment is not brief: it takes more than a hundred lines, nearly a tenth of the whole play, from the entrance of Heracles with the veiled woman until he persuades Admetus to take her by the hand. For some viewers and readers, no amount of persuasion should suffice to accomplish this, for with this gesture—a key part of Greek marriage—Admetus violates at least the spirit of his promise never to remarry. Yet Heracles' insistence, it seems, succeeds in converting funeral into wedding, death into renewed life, and restoring both husband and wife to their proper spatial spheres.

Parents and Children

In the *Alcestis* Euripides tests the categories of parent and child just as much as he does those of husband and wife. The play takes care to stage the visual ideal of a family, only to destroy it minutes later. When Alcestis emerges from the house at line 244, she is accompanied not only by her husband Admetus but her children as well. Neither child is identified by name in this play, though other sources (which do not harmonize easily with each other) name the son Eumelus, leader of the Pheraeans at Troy (Hom. *Il.* 2.715ff.), and the daughter Perimele, either wife or mother of Argus, builder of the Argo for Jason (first mentioned in Hesiod's *Catalogue of Women*).[18] The son sings a moving lament over his mother and so is organic to the drama, but the daughter is only a silent presence. Alcestis' prayer to Hestia to grant both her children happy marriages, reported by the Servant at 165–6, first alerts the audience to the daughter's existence, but the appearance of a female child onstage is rare. Her presence therefore functions not so much to remind the audience of her specific role in later myth as to increase the pathos of the death scene as both children are deprived of their mother.

Untimely as the death of Alcestis is, the expected course of nature is for parents to die before their children. Admetus, however, though head of his household and a ruling king, is the child of still-living parents. His father Pheres, like Cadmus in Euripides' *Bacchae* or Laertes in the *Odyssey*, has given up the kingship to his son but still expects to be treated as a father—precisely what Admetus angrily rejects.

Just as he promised Alcestis to become both mother and father to their children (377), so now Admetus sees himself virtually as the adopted child of Alcestis; he considers her both his mother *and* his father (646–7).[19] In actual Greek practice, only a father could adopt. Luschnig even notes a striking gender reversal in the language of the play when Admetus uses the masculine gender to refer to Alcestis in lines 667–8, something no literary translation into English can preserve: "I say I am that [masculine] one's (*keinou*) child and caretaker in old age."[20] Most striking is Admetus' image of himself as the "caretaker in old age" (*gêrotrophos*) of Alcestis; such care was the duty of the child to the parent and was often cited explicitly as a motivation for someone without children to adopt.[21] Adoption by a new father, however, had as a necessary concomitant severance of the relationship between natural (biological) father and son. Pheres has refused to make the sacrifice that would perpetuate the *oikos* of Admetus and Alcestis. He has put himself before the claims of Admetus' house, and that house rejects him in return. Admetus transfers all his filial duty from Pheres to Alcestis and the house that she died for.[22]

It would be easy, but quite wrong, to burlesque Admetus' declaration here: out of context, his promise to be Alcestis' "caretaker in old age" may seem absurd because she is already dead. The point rather emphasizes his complete break with Pheres: a natural father no longer has any claim on his biological son once that son has been adopted by another, to whom all loyalty and duty are now owed.

The language of fathers and sons is always ideologically powerful, even when forces work to suppress it, as contemporary Greek political practice showed. Key in the development of Athens' democratic civic ideology in the fifth century is a new way of naming citizens in public contexts. In the democracy a man is no longer identified by a patronymic, that is, by a name marking him as the son of another man. Instead, as the eloquent casualty lists marking the mounting costs of the Athenian empire show, a man is now known only by his name and tribe, his identity fixed by his place in the Cleisthenic organization of the city.[23] So too Admetus' house disavows the patronymic in the person of Pheres.

This angry wrangle conducted over the very corpse of Alcestis still dismays modern readers and audiences even more than it does the chorus, which reproves both father and son (673–4; 706–7).[24] An age of individualism can see both men here as equally self-interested, equally unheroic. Attempting to use a fifth-century lens to view their behavior may shift our perspective a bit. Nearly contemporary with this play is a fundamental discussion of death and the value of sacrifice in the funeral oration of Pericles, as reported by the historian Thucydides. In it, Pericles offers counsel to the fathers of warriors who have died for Athens. Those who can beget more sons to defend the city, should do so; otherwise:

> those of you who have passed your prime must congratulate yourselves with the thought that the best part of your life was fortunate, and that the brief span that remains will be cheered by the fame of the departed.
> Thucydides 2. 44. 4[25]

Pericles does not contemplate the possibility that those past their prime could have died on the field in place of their sons; rather, their comfort must be in the fame of their children's sacrifice. Pheres sees no fame for either Alcestis or Admetus in her sacrifice, only pure utility. An Athenian public that approved of Pericles' sentiments might find Pheres unduly self-interested.

Xenia, Philia, and *Charis*

The *Alcestis* is deeply concerned with the connections and distinctions between two profoundly important concepts and value systems in Greek culture: *xenia* (hospitality or guest friendship) and *philia* (personal friendship, affection, and at times love). Both may be regarded anthropologically as systems of exchange, binding the participants together. Individual instances or acts of either friendship or hospitality may both be designated a *charis* (favor). Moreover, the boundaries between the two are permeable, at least in one direction: a *xenos* (stranger/guest) may become a *philos* (friend) in time.[26]

Zeus Xenios presided over the sacred institution of *xenia* or guest-friendship, a practice already seen fully developed in Homer. Receiving a stranger or visitor into one's home created mutual obligations, which might even be heritable.[27] Many interpretations of this play, particularly those which seek even a modicum of sympathy for Admetus, focus on the importance of *xenia*. As Apollo in the prologue tells how Zeus condemned him to serve the mortal Admetus as a laborer, he calls Admetus his *xenos* (6), his host in the guest-friend relationship. Admetus' kind treatment of him has created a reciprocal obligation. The word *hosios* in line 10 of Apollo's speech is particularly difficult to translate for modern audiences. It generally means "holy," though many translators shy away from this here, when Apollo says "I, being *hosios* myself, encountered a *hosios* man, the son of Pheres." The use of the same term for both god and man in a single line suggest a startling equivalency, at least in terms of their relationship; however translated, it implies that both were capable of and did recognize a mutual sense of sacred obligation. For this reason, Apollo has tricked the Fates and obtained for Admetus the opportunity to substitute another's death for his own.

This theme of *xenia* thus looks forward, even explicitly, to Admetus' reception of his guest-friend Heracles into his house, which will in turn prompt Heracles to rescue Alcestis. Apollo's parting speech proclaims that someone will come from Thrace and, having been entertained (*xenotheis*, 68) in the halls of Admetus, will take Alcestis away from Death by force. On an abstract level, then, the abundant *xenia* that the chorus praises in the third stasimon (568) begets *xenia*, and the initial crisis created by Apollo's response is resolved by the intervention of Heracles.

The relationship between host and guest can go horribly wrong, a specter raised briefly in Heracles' first scene. Heracles' first word on arrival addresses the *xenoi* (476) of the chorus. Here the word means "strangers," the mutual position from which guests and host begin. As soon as Heracles states his mission, the chorus demonstrates its good intent toward him by its warning that he is unfamiliar with the nature of his future *xenos* (484), Diomedes, the owner of the man-eating horses that he must bring back. Their description of the host who turns his guests into horse-fodder in part characterizes the power of Heracles as hero, but it also illustrates the violent state of nature, red in tooth and hoof, which is the antitype of *xenia*.[28] With the appearance of Admetus and the discussion of whether Heracles will remain as a guest or go to another host, the scene works to re-establish Admetus and Heracles as guest-friends. Admetus' very last word to Heracles is that there should be no suffering for his guests (*xenous*, 550).

While not all guest-friendships become friendships in the more personal sense, it is worth noting those that do. Admetus is more than Apollo's host: he is also explicitly Apollo's friend (*philou*, 42), just as his house is most dear (*philtatên*, 23) to the god. The emotional aspects of *philia* therefore intertwine with the structural obligations of *xenia*—but are by no means congruent. The word *philia* itself is unknown in Homer and uncommon before the time of Euripides' plays.[29] While significantly more frequent in Euripides than the other two tragedians, *philia* and its related forms cover not only guest-friendships and political alliances, rulers and ruled (the chorus addresses Admetus as "friend to friend," *philos philôi*, 369), but also what we would think of as the more private and intimate relationships of husbands and wives, parents and children, even masters and servants.

These relationships in turn entail more than private emotional affinities between individuals; they too are characterized by mutual obligation and exchange. Begging her not to yield and die, Admetus tells Alcestis that he and the children "honor your love" (*sên gar philian sebomestha*, 279),[30] the *philia* which seems to hold their family and house together. The chorus will later say that, in dying, Alcestis has left *philia* behind (930).[31] Alcestis takes Admetus' love for their children as a given ("you love them," *phileis*, 302). In return for her sacrifice, Alcestis asks Admetus never to remarry and to preserve their children as masters in the household. While we cannot precisely reconstruct the staging here, some specific action or gesture acknowledging the obligation seems implied by this key exchange:

> Alc. On these conditions, receive these children from my hand.
> Adm. I receive them, a dear (*philon*) gift from a dear (*philês*) hand.
>
> (375–6)

Admetus' words express not just his emotion, but his sense that their children and his future treatment of them embody the *philia* he shares with his wife.

Alcestis calls her sacrifice a favor or gift (*charis*, 299), which can never really be repaid.[32] A *charis* can be given or refused, and one choice or the other embodies friendship—or hatred. Apollo asks Death to give him the *charis* (60) of sparing Alcestis' life. Refused, Apollo calls Death hateful to gods and men alike (62) and declares he will be forced to yield in the end anyway—but then it will be no *charis* (70). When Pheres comes, bearing gifts for Alcestis' funeral, Admetus angrily rejects them; there are to be no further exchanges between those who are now enemies to each other. With bitter sarcasm Admetus mocks "such a *charis*" (660) as Pheres and his wife gave him, in return for his previously dutiful treatment of them, by refusing to die for him.

It is even possible, in refusing to grant one *charis*, to bestow another of even greater weight and obligation. Once Heracles learns that Admetus and his household are in mourning for this unnamed woman who has been living there, he tells his friend that he will regard it as a thousand-fold *charis* (544) to be allowed to go and stay with another of his friends in Pherae.[33] When the servant reveals how he has been deceived, Heracles decides he must repay the *charis* (842) of Admetus by rescuing Alcestis from Death, the master of corpses, whether at the tomb or even by going down into the underworld. Having done so, he deceives his host in turn, at least for a time, when he wishes out loud that he had had the power to bring Alcestis back from the dead to Admetus—and grant him this *charis* (1074).

A key question is whether Admetus regards Heracles from the beginning as a *philos* as well as a *xenos*. When the chorus questions Admetus' actions in welcoming Heracles into his house, they ask how he can do this to "an arriving friend, as you yourself say" (*philou molontos andros hôs autos legeis*, 562). As G. R. Stanton points out,[34] however, they are slightly misquoting Admetus back to himself; Admetus just a few lines before spoke of Heracles as his "arriving guest" (*xenon molonta*, 554), and both Heracles and Admetus used only the term *xenos* of their relation to each other in the preceding dialogue (e.g. 540, 550). Only on his return with the veiled woman does Heracles explicitly stake his claim to be a friend and to be treated as a friend (*philon*, 1008; *philos*, 1011) by Admetus—and then praises Admetus as a faithful friend (*philos*, 1095) to his late wife.[35] Heracles suggests that Admetus' treatment of him in concealing the truth has not allowed him to be tested as a friend, and he should have been afforded that opportunity. The entire scene then is framed as Heracles' response to the belatedly discovered test.

All of this, however, begs the question of whether these various acts of *charis* can and should be freely exchanged. The social value of gift exchange is to promote a sense of cohesion among the participants—but cohesion repeatedly fails in this play. Apollo's original act of *charis* exposes how fundamentally gods and men differ. Unless we are to take Pheres' bitter sneers as literal truth (and nothing in the play suggests we should), Apollo's gift is not an unlimited license for Admetus to find an endless series of substitutes to die for him, whenever death threatens; avoiding his death at one moment in time does not make him immortal like the gods. Alcestis' gift is similarly unreciprocable: far from making immortal the household for which she dies, her death destroys it. Apollo's gift is so large that it breaks down the system of exchange, and so too does that of Alcestis.[36] Admetus wishes that he could die with her (382) and must be prevented from hurling himself in the grave with her body (897–8), but even his death cannot repay hers. In a structural sense, only the hero Heracles, mortal offspring of Zeus and Alcmene who eventually becomes immortal, can mediate here by operating on both divine and human levels.

Alcestis herself is a *charis*, both object and subject in various systems of exchange. Although Euripides has suppressed all details of the betrothal story, her father originally gave Alcestis away in marriage—and if we are meant to know, only unwillingly, to the one suitor, Admetus, who with Apollo's help yoked a lion and boar together to a chariot. Once married, Alcestis gives herself away as a bride to Death, in order to save her children, her house, and her husband. Finally Heracles reclaims her back as a prize and gives her back again to Admetus—at which point the exchanges finally cease.

Life and Death

> Adm. One about to die, even though present, no longer exists.
> Her. Being and non-being are considered separate things.
> Adm. You think of this in one way, Heracles, and I in another.
>
> (527–9)

These lines are usually identified as the key moment in the play at which Admetus deceives his friend Heracles, playing sophistic word games to suggest that Alcestis is alive, when in fact she is dead. Heard in isolation, Admetus' words are a contemptible falsehood, an affront alike to friendship and the memory of his dead wife. In form, however, they offer one of the most characteristic forms of Euripides' sophistic play with words and categories (something is "X and not X," "X and un-X") that Aristophanes loved to parody.[37] When her husband says that Alcestis is both alive and not alive, Heracles and most members of an audience will instinctively resist this claim—how can this most fundamental opposition be denied or evaded?

Yet Euripides has already prepared the ground, and throughout this play he rings many changes both obvious and subtle on the ambiguities of this apparently irreconcilable opposition. The chorus arrives wondering whether Alcestis is alive or dead—and the servant's very first words state the ambiguity concretely: "You could say she is both living and dead" (141). Much more delicate yet equally unsettling are Admetus' words that begin his promise to Alcestis in their farewell scene:

> Just as I held you
> when you were living, so also, having died, you alone
> will be called my wife …
>
> (328–30)

The participles in the Greek here are subordinate to the tenses of the main verbs. When Admetus says "I held you" (a verb also implying their marriage bond), the past tense implies his holding her is over—even though the actor may be physically holding the other actor playing Alcestis even as he speaks this line. The future tense in "you will be called my wife," however, as Mary Stieber points out, echoes the formulaic language of archaic funerary inscriptions, such as the famous epitaph of Phrasikleia: "I shall always be called a maiden, having been allotted this name by the gods in place of a marriage."[38] Admetus thus speaks to his wife as though she were already dead and the subject of her posthumous fame.

The language of Greek epitaphs, on which this play had an important influence (see Chapter 4, below), offers parallels for the metaphoric if not literal interchange of life and death, including one likely to have been familiar to many in Euripides' audience. A verse epitaph composed for the Athenian fallen at the battle of Platea in the Persian War and attributed to the poet Simonides says:

> These men crowned their country with glory
> and were gathered into the darkness of death.
> They died, but are not dead (*oude tethnasi, thanontes*); their courage
>   (*aretê*)
> brings them back in glory from the world below.
>   (trans. William Arrowsmith)[39]

With characteristic irony, Euripides inverts the order: after their sacrifice the heroes of Plataea are both dead and returned, but Alcestis is both present and already departed before hers.

Lament

As the proverbial phrase "nothing to do with Dionysus" shows, the Greeks themselves debated how or whether the dramas staged in honor of Dionysus had meaning as religious ritual for their audiences.

Whatever the conclusion, it is nonetheless clear that Attic theater could incorporate or represent other rituals within its own structure. One of the most widespread is the ritual of lament. How do we know a lament when we hear one? It is most useful to consider lament not just as any expression of mourning or grief, but as a formal structure with linguistic and metrical features that would evoke or resonate with ritual lament as practiced in the society of the contemporary Athenian audience. Though we can clearly identify some Greek terms (*goos*, individual lament; *thrênos*, choral lament; *kommos*, a structure of *goos* and *thrênos* in responsion), no ancient source tells us exactly what ritual lament entailed. A comparison of passages in a number of tragedies can nonetheless offer plausible criteria for identifying lament on the Attic stage by formal features of language and metrical change. The clearest examples occur at the ends of tragedies, such as Xerxes and the chorus' lament for the Persian dead at the end of Aeschylus' *Persians* or Creon and the chorus' lament for his dead son Haemon at the end of Sophocles' *Antigone*. These are "full" laments, but "reduced" versions appear at earlier points in plays as well.[40]

While expressions of sorrow occur throughout the *Alcestis*, three passages in particular evince the formal features as well as typical themes of lament: the son's lament over his dead mother's body (393–415), the chorus' parting lament as they exit with the body in the funeral cortege (741–6), and the responsive lament of Admetus and the chorus after their return from the graveside (861–933).[41] Given the association of the fully developed lament with the ending of tragedy, each of these laments creates at least some sense of closure to a part of the action. After their son's lyric lament, Admetus gives his commands for mourning and then accompanies his wife's body into the palace. The stage is left vacant for the first time since the prologue. The short choral lament at 741–6 accompanies the *ekphora*, the departure of the body from the house for burial, and leaves behind both an empty stage and an empty orchestra. Given their brevity, neither of these laments can have created in the audience an expectation that the play was truly over, but both create a temporary rest.

The lament shared by Admetus and the chorus on their return from the graveside (861–933) is potentially more deceptive. It is as long as or longer than some "full" laments which close other plays.[42] A satyr play was regularly shorter than the preceding members of a tetralogy, and the original audience for the *Alcestis* might well think that they were getting close to the end of the play by line 933. Yet subtle formal signals might also alert the audience that this is not a standard final lament—and therefore perhaps not the play's last word. Admetus sings his part in the lament in anapaestic meter; normally it is the chorus that sings anapaests in a lament. In this exchange, however, the chorus sings in iambic and dactylic rhythms. Moreover, the order in which the chorus usually sings these differing meters is here reversed: where most laments move from dactylic to often highly resolved iambic rhythms, with a sense of increasing speed and emotion, here the movement is in the opposite direction.[43] Thus the language of mourning at this point in the play and the length at which it is expressed together suggest a sense of an ending, while the musical form, reversing the standard assignment of meters and the usual direction of development, simultaneously undercuts a sense of closure.

Lament possesses not just an emotional and therapeutic function but a cultural one as well. Within the poetic form of tragedy, lament not only expresses the grief natural to the characters in the situation but also contributes to the celebration of the *kleos* or glory of those for whom they mourn. At Admetus' command (423–4), the chorus had earlier sung an ode that both itself celebrated Alcestis' glory and promised future ritual repetition of hymns glorifying her (*kleontes humnois*, 447) both in Athens and Sparta. Thus the celebration of the glory she earns by death precedes within the play the fullest lament offered for her and one described self-consciously by Admetus as the *goos* (922) that accompanies him, even as he takes part in it.

The three laments thus close three sections of the play, none of which is really the ending—and all of which are profoundly revised by the final section.

Fame and Infamy

Characters and chorus alike praise the nobility of Alcestis' sacrifice over and over and promise her lasting fame for her deed. She is included among the *agathoi* ("noble," 109; 745) and repeatedly called *aristê* ("the best [of women]"). While the masculine superlative *aristos* is quite common from Homer onward, very few women are accorded this title; *aristê* never is used of a woman in Pindar or Aeschylus, and only three times in Sophocles, but this play calls Alcestis *aristê* nine different times.[44] Alcestis is also called *eukle*ês ("glorious") by both the chorus (150, coupled with *aristê* at 151) and her husband (938), and even Pheres at first says his daughter-in-law "made life for all women more glorious" (*eukleesteron*, 623) by her sacrifice. Her virtue is moreover recognized by the whole city (156). All of this praise is grounded in action: Alcestis is noble *because* she dies.

By contrast, both Alcestis and Admetus portray his parents' refusal to die for him as infamous. Alcestis asserts that the parents could have died "gloriously" (*eukleos*, 292) to save their son—but did not. Admetus insists his father will die "dishonored" (*duskleês*, 725) when he does leave this life, and Pheres replies that he does not care if men speak ill of him, once he is dead (726). For all that both men come off badly in their quarrel over the very corpse of Alcestis, Pheres' is the distinctly unheroic point of view; he rejects the whole system of *kleos* and the notion of posthumous fame for which heroes strive.

The play's praise of Alcestis is grounded within a larger chain of actions. Since it is the result of her own choice, Alcestis' death is in one sense a suicide, in another a human sacrifice on behalf of the *oikos*. Yet her suicide, if we are to classify it as such, is like no other in Greek tragedy. Nicole Loraux's litany of the *Tragic Ways of Killing a Woman* includes appropriate and inappropriate suicide methods.[45] There are feminine and non-feminine forms of lethal violence visited upon the female body—but that of which Alcestis dies occurs nowhere else in ancient drama. She seems simply to fade away. In fact, one might argue that the apparent naturalness of Alcestis' onstage death is an unrecognized source of generic unease, of the feeling that *Alcestis* is somehow a comedy or at least a melodrama rather than a tragedy. The violent deaths of tragedy are kept offstage, but in comedy characters can slip softly but visibly away.[46] Precisely because she dies not by the noose or the blade, Alcestis is set apart from all those other women who tread the way to death in Greek tragedy.

Death masculinizes Alcestis. She will have the public reputation a man should. Released from the women's quarters, she will have a name and honor in the public realm. Indeed, it has been suggested that Euripides has specifically modeled elements of her portrayal on the heroism of Patroclus and Hector in Homer's *Iliad*.[47] Paradoxically, the lack of violence in her death is a part of this heroic masculinity. Emily Vermeule has shown how death in epic poetry feminizes the male warrior, rendering the strong, hard body soft, pliable, capable of being pierced and controlled.[48] Alcestis alone among women in Greek tragedy dies intact.

This masculine element in Alcestis and her sacrifice comes into even sharper relief when we look at the performative context of the play, at its place within the Great Dionysia. Simon Goldhill has drawn attention to elements of the festival celebration which preceded the actual performance of the plays and has used these elements as a horizon against which to read the contents of some tragedies, notably Sophocles' *Ajax* and *Philoctetes*. In his view these other, non-dramatic elements of the festival praise the city and offer a unified celebration of Athens, but tragedy and comedy both function as transgressive genres within the festival, offering an interrogation of the festival's otherwise uniform praise of civic ideology. Mark Griffith,[49] among others, has argued that civic ideology was not quite as monophonic as Goldhill suggests. The *Alcestis* in particular may offer an interesting counter-example to some of Goldhill's general claims.

Goldhill points to four elements in particular in the ceremonies of the Dionysia as festival celebrations of Athens' power and self-confidence: the ten generals offered libations; the tribute from the allies was displayed; crowns were awarded to citizens; and finally, war orphans, who had been nurtured by the state because their fathers had died in battle and had now reached maturity, paraded in the orchestra and received military equipment. These newly enrolled citizen warriors or ephebes were then led to seats of honor in the theater (*proedria*) to watch the plays.

What we know of the bestowing of civic crowns in the theater during the festival derives largely from the dispute a century later between two Athenian politicians, Aeschines and Demosthenes, over the award of a crown to the latter. Demosthenes (*On the Crown*, 120) makes the claim that the award of such a crown in so public a ceremony really honors the generosity of the city as donor, a view Goldhill essentially accepts:

> [T]his ceremony was perceived as an important public occasion. The proclamation of the names of those who had benefited the city was another way of asserting the ties, connections, and duties between individuals and the city.[50]

Goldhill sees the awarding of the crowns as a celebration of the city and a positive reinforcement of civic ideology; all the pre-play ceremonies then offer a foil to the more "questioning" and "transgressive" plays that followed.[51]

Demosthenes' opponent Aeschines has a different, much less binary view, and the specifics of his argument repay closer attention.

Aeschines claims that only crowns awarded by foreign powers may, with the permission of the demos, be given in the theater, whereas awards by the city must be given in the assembly (*In Ctes*, 41–7). This sounds like a technicality, and Aeschines is scarcely an impartial witness. Nonetheless, the international audience at the City Dionysia was the obvious venue for the Athenian demos to cooperate with foreign states in bestowing awards.[52] Moreover, Aeschines presents a much more chaotic view of what happened at the festival preceding the plays at some earlier, unspecified time. Unlike the practice in his own time, at an earlier (possibly fifth-century) period various groups and individuals within Athens used the festival as a platform to make public proclamations of praise—sometimes engineered by the individual recipients themselves.[53] In short, at some point in the past, the Dionysia was much more chaotic and indeed not completely in control of the state.[54]

Praise then was something of a laissez-faire free-for-all. Our evidence for blame, however, is that it was indeed in the control of the state, for the proclamations sponsored by the state were not solely positive and prescriptive. From Aristophanes' *Birds* we have evidence of the proclamation of rewards for killing the enemies of the state:

> It's proclaimed on this day in particular:
> "If any of you kills Diagoras the Melian,
> he'll receive one talent, and if anyone kills
> one of the dead tyrants, he'll receive a talent."
>
> (*Birds*, 1072–5)

Diagoras the Melian fled Athens to avoid prosecution for atheism, and a reward for his return dead or alive was unsuccessfully offered, no later than about 417.[55] A curse against tyrants and their supporters was also pronounced at all meetings of the Assembly,[56] another element that links the Assembly to the "politics by other means" of the Dionysiac festivals. In other words, the ceremonies of the

Dionysia reinforced civic ideology both by the carrot and by the stick—even when the sticks were so outdated that Aristophanes can make fun of the notion of killing the dead tyrants.

The fact that the official ceremonies included both praise and blame is significant for the relation of the plays to overall civic ideology. The proclamations both cajole and decry: they are not monophonic civic praise. The plays too, then, may mix their messages; if the ceremonies are not pure propaganda background, neither need the plays be as uniformly "trangressive" or "questioning" of shared civic values.

The parade of the war orphans was clearly one of the most moving and most important elements of the pre-play ceremonies.[57] Structurally the counterpoint to the display of the allied tributes, the parade was the site of much more complex emotions. After viewing the rewards of empire, the city contemplated the costs, both mourning its losses and congratulating itself at the same time on its care for the sons of those fallen in battle. The parade of orphans was also, at least on one occasion in the fifth century, the arena of struggle over the notions of citizenship and heritage. At the very end of the century, Lysias attacked Theozotides for a proposal to exclude adopted and illegitimate sons from this ceremony. The motivation for Theozotides' proposal seems to have been financial, but the emotion of Lysias' response testifies to the importance of this ceremony in particular to the city.[58] For Lysias at least, any differentiation in the treatment of the sons of the fallen was a threat to both the unity and the generosity of the city.

One could hardly find a tragedy in which the fate of orphaned children and the value of the sacrifice made on their behalf was more intimately involved than *Alcestis*. The celebration of the state as parent in the pre-play ceremonies of the Dionysia provides an immediate and compelling frame through which to view Alcestis, her sacrifice, and the fate of her children.

Nicole Loraux's *The Invention of Athens* illuminates the Athenian view of the soldiers who made the ultimate sacrifice on its behalf.[59]

As she demonstrates, the institution of the public funeral oration (*epitaphios*) and the erection by the state of casualty lists attest to the growth of a civic ideology which identifies the state as the object of loyalty and sacrifice, at the same time subordinating grief for the individual dead to celebration of the glory of the whole city.[60] Moreover, that state becomes the father and mother of the citizens, and violence against the state a form of parricide; at least from Pericles' citizenship law of 451/0 onward, the state begins to co-opt the language of family relations.[61]

Dying to preserve her house, Alcestis entrusts her children to Admetus who is to be both father and mother to them. It has even been suggested that the audience might see this as an adoption ceremony, although we know essentially nothing of the rituals of Greek adoption at this period.[62] The parallel, however, of these apparently private actions to those of the Athenian state as represented in the ceremony of the orphans is striking—as is the gender reversal. A man becomes *agathos* by dying in battle for the city;[63] in return, the city raises his sons and outfits them as new warriors to defend and perpetuate the city. Alcestis through her sacrifice becomes *agathê* and entrusts her children to Admetus to raise and perpetuate the *oikos*.

In *Alcestis*, then, the royal *oikos* functions as a metonym for the city. This is a nuclear *oikos*, cut off from more extended personal ties. When Admetus denies the existence of any further tie to his father, he is simply acknowledging what is already the case: his house is cut off from any more extended family and turns in upon itself. Alcestis has already demonstrated this when she prepares both the house and her own body for death (cf. lines 158–61)—tasks that the next of kin would normally undertake after a death.[64]

The language of the play frames Alcestis' sacrifice as virtuous and glorious. Even Pheres, the least sympathetic audience for her decision, acknowledges the glory (623), even if he questions the rationality of her decision (calling her "not shameless ... but senseless" [*ouk anaides … aphrona*, 728]). Her sacrifice stakes an unrefuted claim to honor and glory in traditionally masculine terms—but the story does not end there. Alcestis does not stay dead, Admetus is not permanently feminized, and her *kleos* may not remain exactly the same.

Doubles and Opposites

The Greeks famously thought in binary oppositions, a pattern for which the Pythagorean Table of Opposites (light and dark, male and female, right and left, and so forth)[65] is the archetype. Though finding examples in Greek literature is therefore an easy task, this play still seems to display an intriguing emphasis on doubling and opposition, both thematically and structurally.

As we have already seen, the play begins with powerful visual and structural oppositions. The confrontation between Apollo and Death pits Olympian against chthonian deity even as it etches the boundaries between inside and outside, mortal and immortal, death and life. The entrance of the chorus draws another opposition, only to erase it soon thereafter. As argued above, the appearance of the chorus of old men (instead of satyrs) was likely a surprise to most in the first audience. These choristers embody a contrast to the expected; where satyrs are hyperbolically masculine figures in their prime, these old men are defined by their lack of vigor. According to the ancient scholiast, there was a further visual surprise: the chorus was divided into two half-choruses, something that happens only rarely in Greek tragedy and never, to our knowledge, for a *parôdos* before this play.[66] The sense of confusion in the audience can only have been increased by the sight of choristers tottering in from both side entrances, probably with individual voices singled out and alternating from sides of the orchestra.[67] The two bodies of singers then merge into one.

The play itself seems to consist of two different songs (*dissa melê*, 760), as the servant puts it when he speaks to the audience over the empty orchestra in what seems to be a second prologue. One is the sound of Heracles singing in revelry (761), the other the weeping of the household in mourning. Divided spatially (one in the guest quarters, the other in the rest of the house), the two songs are not temporally so easily divided. Though all preceding this point has been a song of mourning, from here on the two songs compete—until Admetus proclaims choruses in honor of good fortune (1155) at the end.

To these doubles of sight and sound may be added those of imagination as well. Alcestis herself is doubled, not just dying and living, beginning and end, but both as enacted and as imagined. A particularly evocative double for Alcestis emerges in Admetus' promise to commission a statue of her.

Alcestis' Statue

In the excess of his grief, Admetus tells Alcestis that he will try to console himself by having an artist sculpt her image. Not only that: he plans to place it in the marital bed that figures so prominently in Alcestis' lament:[68]

> Your image (*demas*), wrought by the skilled hand of craftsmen
>   (*tektonôn*),
> shall lie in our bed, and I
> shall fall on it and clasp my arms about it.
> Calling your name, I shall seem to hold
> my dear wife in my embrace—though I do not.
>
> (348–52)

If we read this image through the lens of stories in later antiquity of those who fell in love with statues (e.g., Praxiteles' famous sculpture of the Aphrodite of Cnidos),[69] it may seem a highly distasteful notion, evoking not so much the artistic creativity of Ovid's Pygmalion as the functionality of a life-size rubber doll. Dale (*ad loc.*) and others have read it rather as an expression of the extravagance of Admetus' grief, and not morbid perversion.

Charles Segal has offered one of the more ambitious attempts to rescue this image from its critics, seeing it as a symbol for mimetic power, including the art of playmaking itself.[70] Drawing on the work of J.-P. Vernant before him, he views the proposed statue as a *kolossos*, supposedly the image in Greek funerary ritual buried as a substitute for a missing body under certain circumstances.[71] This proposed *kolossos* also then anticipates the empty grave at the end of the play, since Alcestis' body will not remain buried.

Such an explanation, linking Admetus' idea to Greek burial practice, offers one horizon of explanation. Yet the evidence for the use of *kolossoi* in burial practice is very early and very thin,[72] and one imagines that few Greeks would have had personal experience of this element of burial ritual in any case. Moreover, even if such *kolossoi* existed, they disappeared from view once used. As such, they do not form a clear visual repertoire for the audience to draw on while interpreting Euripides.

The modern world is flooded with images of specific individuals, the vast majority produced by photographic processes. Paintings and sculptures are much rarer, but by no means unknown. Ancient Athens was very different.

What sculpted images of specific human beings would an Athenian in 438 BC have seen? A century before, the practice of carving idealized representations of the young had been prevalent. Many statues of young women (now termed *korai*) and some of young men (*kouroi*) had been dedicated on the Athenian Acropolis, but after the Persian invaders destroyed it in 480 BC, the shattered remnants had been cleared away, and a new, much less cluttered Acropolis was rising above the theater. In the Athens of 438, only those statues commemorating the dead remained. A very few honored the heroic dead, such as the statues of the tyrant-slayers Harmodius and Aristogeiton in the Agora. The Persians had stolen the original statues, and newly carved replacements now stood in their place. Elsewhere, the aristocratic dead, whose families could afford to honor them so, were commemorated by funerary *kouroi* and *korai* (as well perhaps as sculpted stelai) from the late sixth and early fifth centuries. Many still stood in the Kerameikos cemetery right outside the city gates and in private funeral plots on family estates in the countryside. Yet funerary statues were no longer being erected when Euripides wrote the *Alcestis*: there seems to have been a ban on any kind of private, individual funerary monument through most of the fifth century down to the outbreak of the Peloponnesian War in 431. As a recent study has pointed out:

> [A]t some time early in the fifth century Athens not only limited what individuals or families could do but instituted state funerals with public orations for the war dead, and as a result largely monopolized public and monumental commemoration on stone between c. 490 and 430.[73]

No member of the original audience would erect a statue of a deceased wife, at least not out in the open; such private heroization was no longer practiced.

The point, though subtle, is this: such images were no longer compatible with the current ideology of the democracy. Here too we see how *Alcestis* plays games of gender reversal with memory and fame. While Admetus proposes the statue as a personal consolation and reminder, an image only for his viewing, hidden away not just in the house but in the marital bedchamber itself,[74] the only parallels that the original audience could visualize existed in public space and honored the male heroic dead, such as the tyrannicides and the aristocratic dead of an earlier period.

Finally, Alcestis' statue is a thought experiment even within the fiction of the play, a proposal only, the need for which is erased by her own return. It is part of the alternate world of female *kleos*, imagined by the initial action of the play and promised to Alcestis by husband and chorus alike, but changed profoundly by her restoration to life at the hands of Heracles.

What, then, is the relationship of this play and its ending to the festival as a whole? Let us recall here Goldhill's claim about the relationship of tragedy in general to the messages of the Dionysia:

> Rather than simply reflecting the cultural values of the fifth-century audience, then, rather than offering simple didactic messages from the city's poets to the citizens, tragedy seems deliberately to make difficult the assumption of the values of the civic discourse.[75]

The choice seems somewhat forced: *either* "simple didactic messages" *or* tragedies that set out to make it difficult for the citizens to believe in the values of the city. There are probably a few more points along the spectrum, and *Alcestis* occupies one of them.

Alcestis' sacrifice on behalf of the *oikos* would evoke the most powerful stimulus to pity in the pre-play ceremonies, the parade of war orphans. Like the fallen fathers of these orphans, she offers her life in defense of her home. Other elements that masculinize her even as they feminize Admetus underscore her role as protector. These parallels would have been even more compelling in performance than they are read from a page—which is not yet to say we know precisely how to interpret them. One could still insist that the ending of the play is bitterly ironic—but if so, the ironies will multiply beyond what has yet been recognized. If Alcestis makes a meaningless sacrifice of herself for an unworthy man, the parallels will open up the question of how *meaningful* have been the sacrifices of all those men who have died for Athens and her empire. Euripides may have been enough of an ironist to ask that question in 438, seven years before the great Peloponnesian War broke out, but it seems doubtful.

Perhaps his experiment in heroic gender reversal is designed rather to make the Athenian audience think in a new way about sacrifice on behalf of both the city and the *oikos*, not with a view toward doubting the value of either, but of appreciating both more deeply. The earliest survivor in the line of Euripides' remarkable heroines displays both a masculine valor and a profoundly feminine devotion to family. A few years later, Euripides' Medea famously weighs the choices of childbearing and standing in the battle line (*Medea*, 250–1). Alcestis chooses both: after risking her life in childbirth, she lays it down on a different battle line, defending the *oikos* of which she has become a part. Her return into the household that she saved does not erase either the fact or the motivation of her sacrifice. Indeed, given that the whole household, including Admetus, is orphaned by her death, only her return can bring immediate restoration—paradoxically, by merging silently back into it. The ironic awareness that, despite their similar cost, male and female self-sacrifice are differently understood and honored in Athens colors, but need not overwhelm, the celebration of the ending.

Marriage, Remarriage—and Silence

A second marriage is the triumph of hope over experience.
Samuel Johnson

Alcestis returns, thanks to the efforts of Heracles (as predicted by Apollo), and, in a visually arresting performance, is "remarried" to Admetus.[76] Interpretation of this scene, in which Heracles persuades Admetus not only to receive the veiled woman that he has won as a "prize" into the house but also to take her personally from Heracles' hand, is at the heart of our understanding of Euripides' play. Some find it unforgivable that, after his pledge to Alcestis, Admetus then admits "another woman" into their home. Others note not only the length of his resistance to Heracles' request (this discussion occupies virtually a tenth of the play) but also the fact that his obedience to the dictates of *xenia* as he understands them reenacts his original hospitality to Apollo, the origin of the whole story (see above).[77]

While the imagined psychology of Admetus and Alcestis in this final scene has greatly interested many critics, less attention has been paid to the social and cultural function of marriage in the fiction of the play. The details Admetus evokes from their original marriage, as he hesitates on the doorstep of the palace, show that Euripides depicts their original union as what sociologists and anthropologists term a "betrothal marriage," freely undertaken and welcomed by both families. Note particularly lines 918–21:

> … a loud-shouting band of revellers followed,
> blessing the dead woman and me,
> saying we were well-born on both sides,
> a couple from the best stock.

When the following throng declares explicitly how well matched the young bridal pair were,[78] it embodies the society around the pair that recognizes and hails the propriety and free consent of this marriage.

When Heracles brings about the remarriage of Admetus and Alcestis, however, this is arguably an "abduction marriage," a theft of the bride from a controlling male figure who resists this marriage. True, the thief in this case has been the bridegroom's friend rather than the bridegroom himself, but such a proceeding would be by no means unknown in Greek culture. Some abduction marriages involved the tacit consent of the woman abducted, but others did not. As Christopher Faraone points out in a discussion of Greek weddings and erotic magic: "in bridal theft … whether the kidnapped girl is willing or not, she usually pretends … to be unwilling … to save face for herself."[79] For the Greek audience, then, the focus will have been on the successful abduction of Alcestis from the hands of Death, and even were she allowed to speak, the audience might not expect to hear how she "really" felt.

Even within the ancient world itself, the power dynamics of marriage and remarriage were not uniformly understood. When Roman couples re-imagined themselves in the roles of Admetus and Alcestis (see Chapter 4, 71–4, below), they visualized their marriage as a more equal union, symbolized by the joining of their right hands (*dextrarum junctio*), which the sculptors of sarcophagi are careful to represent. This was not necessarily the Greek ideology of marriage. The evidence of other Greek texts and vase paintings suggests that in Greek marriage ritual, the bridegroom used his right hand to grasp the left hand or wrist of the bride. Suppliants in the Greek ritual relationship sought to grasp the right hand of the person supplicated, and some Greeks at least therefore saw "close parallels between raising a supplicant and leading a bride."[80]

Viewed in this way, at first glance the remarriage of Alcestis and Admetus may be even more likely to unsettle modern spectators and readers. Structurally, the veiled woman is indeed in a suppliant position. Her silent presence asks for Admetus' protection in Heracles' imminent absence. Yet how can we see her, once revealed as Alcestis, as a suppliant to the man who owes her everything? The answer, uncongenial as it may be to contemporary sensibilities, may lie in the connotations of a successful supplication, as this proves to be. As Elizabeth Belfiore puts in generally:

> Just as the gesture of taking the suppliant by the hand indicated not dominance and aggression, but *aidôs* and protection, so the same gesture of the husband would have indicated respectful guardianship.[81]

Admetus unknowingly receives the suppliant woman, just as he once received Apollo. The irony, even absurdity of the mortal king treating the unrecognized god with kindness and grace is not so apparent because it is not enacted before us (though see below on Thornton Wilder's treatment). It is only reported in a narrative that already implicitly accepts it as a good thing. The visual irony of treating Alcestis as a suppliant is put before our eyes, and the mind gropes for an evaluative frame. Dispute between what Bradley has labeled ironic and typological views of the play[82] has continued, because the one voice within the play we feel could authoritatively judge Admetus' actions remains silent.

The silence of Alcestis fascinates us. It is intriguing from a performative point of view alone: there are three actors onstage, and only two speak. When Aeschylus produced his *Oresteia* trilogy, he employed three actors. In the middle play, the *Libation Bearers*, however, he accustoms his audience to think that Orestes' friend Pylades is played by a silent extra, because he never speaks—until the crucial moment when, as Orestes hesitates to kill his mother Clytemnestra, Pylades suddenly breaks his silence and urges him on to the killing. By contrast, the end of the *Alcestis* displays what Sherlock Holmes would call the "curious incident of the dog in the night-time."[83] Three speaking actors are available. Probably the same actor who spoke and sang Alcestis' part before her death is now wearing her mask and costume on the stage in this last scene. Once Alcestis is unveiled, there seems to be an expectation of dialogue.[84] Why does she not speak? Admetus want to know:

> Adm. Why ever does the woman stand there speechless?
> Her. It is not yet right for you to hear her utterances.
>
> (1143–5)

Heracles' reply does not suggest, as many translators wrongly imply, that she is incapable of speaking at this moment, but only that it is not yet time for Admetus to hear what she has to say.[85] A psychologically based interpretation of the scene might well ask the question, what on earth *would* she say to Admetus? "Hello, dear, how was *your* day?" It would take the sensibility of a Kleist—or an Aristophanes—to write that particular domestic scene.[86] Movement and gesture can impose a meaning (the actor playing Alcestis can either spurn or embrace Admetus), but while few crucial movements or gestures in a Greek play are left completely unmarked in the play's dialogue, no textual clue here tells us precisely how the silent Alcestis played this scene.

Did the audience of the original production go home thinking that Alcestis' silence was a pregnant one? It may rather have been a gracious silence.[87] For we should note that it is not her silence alone. Not only does she fail to speak, but the chorus of voices around her that had so persistently praised her, proclaimed her *kleos*, and insisted on the lasting quality of her fame has now fallen silent too. Instead, in what Helene Foley has pointed out is virtually a "comedy of remarriage," to borrow Stanley Cavell's term,[88] Alcestis is reunited with her husband and resubmerged in the silence, both objective and subjective, that was the glory of the Athenian wife.

Perhaps some speculation on Alcestis' costume is in order here, for costume can have profound meaning in performance. Her basic costume seems to have been white, facilitating an ambiguity between funeral and marriage.[89] Yet even if she is veiled, why does Admetus not recognize her by her costume (i.e., garment and accoutrements)? She went to her grave splendidly arrayed in her own jewelry and adornments, as we learn from her servant (*kosmos*, 149; *esthêta*, *kosmon*, 161). Later Admetus will angrily reject any other such gifts to adorn her body from Pheres (*kosmon*, 613, 618, 631). Finally, Admetus will determine by her costume (*esthêti kai kosmoi*, 1050) that the woman Heracles presents him with is young.

Marriage is a powerful cultural assertion and demonstration of both masculinity and femininity. In this sense, then, the ending of the *Alcestis* restores both Admetus and Alcestis to their proper gender roles. At the same time, marriage is an essential rite of passage that secures a completed adult status in the community for both participants. Remarriage restores Admetus' masculinity and adulthood as well as his shattered household, which can now be successfully reintegrated into the larger community of his loyal followers at Pherae. Concomitant with the restoration of Admetus' proper gender role as husband in the household is Alcestis' restoration to a more culturally appropriate femininity: she becomes the ideal woman praised by Pericles in his funeral oration (Thucydides 2.35–46), spoken of publicly neither for good nor ill. The word *kosmos* in Greek is multivalent: it means both costume and glory. As Guilia Sissa points out,[90] the true glory of an Athenian woman is silence. The vocal Alcestis of the first part of the play has returned in a new costume: she wears the silence of the modest Athenian wife.

Are we to regard *that* as the real tragedy, the return of Alcestis to such a husband as Admetus? Through the reported words of Alcestis in her farewell to her house and bed we have seen her strong attachment to her role as wife which she gives up through her choice to die for Admetus (the role she regains at the end of the play), and she certainly does not find death preferable to life with Admetus as she speaks that farewell. There is, then, at least one irony *not* present at the end of this play: as Michael Lloyd so penetratingly points out, contrasting Alcestis with Macaria, Polyxena, Iphigenia, and other characters in Euripides who *do* find death the better option, "The happy ending would be rather ironic if Alcestis had gone to her death with the relish of some of the other characters and then had to live again."[91] By the play's own standards, then, this is a happy ending.

4

Afterlives of an Afterlife

To die will be an awfully big adventure.
Peter, in J. M. Barrie's *Peter Pan*

Alcestis has enjoyed a long afterlife, both as a myth and as a performance. It is often not easy to determine whether a particular literary or artistic version of her story comes from the general mythic tradition or specifically from Euripides' play, but the story and the plight of its characters have had an enduring emotional appeal. The afterlives of Alcestis are many, revealing as much about those who pass on her story as they do about her own.

In Antiquity

One version of Alcestis' story enjoyed a vigorous life in performance—though not dramatic performance—well before Euripides put her on stage. Her story formed the theme of a scolion or drinking song, which was often performed at the symposium. The symposium or formal drinking party was an important institution for the formation and transmission of poetry and cultural values in late archaic and early classical Greece. Two verses of this song have come down to us under the name of the poet Praxilla:

> Having learned Admetus' story, comrade, love (*philei*) good men,
> but avoid cowards, knowing that the grace (*charis*) of cowards is
>   meager.
>
> Praxilla 3[1]

The original song was certainly longer than these two preserved verses, but just how much of the story it told is unclear. What it does show is that the story of Alcestis and Admetus was already seen as dealing in themes of goodness and cowardice—even if we cannot say whether the cowardly in its version was exemplified by Admetus or his parents.[2] Particularly noteworthy is that this song was regularly called "Admetus' story" (*Admêtou logos*) or "Admetus' song" (*Admêtou melos*); its focalization therefore seems to have been, for better or worse, on his choices and actions.

Alcestis' story features in Plato's great dialogue on love, the *Symposium*, where Phaedrus, one of the guests, cites her example as one willing to die for love:

> Love will make men dare to die for their beloved—love alone; and women as well as men. Of this, Alcestis, the daughter of Pelias, is a monument to all Hellas; for she was willing to lay down her life on behalf of her husband, when no one else would, although he had a father and mother; but the tenderness of her love so far exceeded theirs, that she made them seem to be strangers in blood to their own son, and in name only related to him; and so noble did this action of hers appear to the gods, as well as to men, that among the many who have done virtuously she is one of the very few to whom, in admiration of her noble action, they have granted the privilege of returning alive to earth; such exceeding honour is paid by the gods to the devotion and virtue of love.
>
> *Symp*. 179bc, trans. B. Jowett

The *Symposium* is set at a party honoring the poet Agathon's victory in a tragic competition about 20 years after Euripides' play was produced. As such, it would seem natural to cite the Euripidean version, but there are both striking inconsistencies as well as similarities. Phaedrus attributes her return from the dead to "the gods," who thus honored her love and devotion. This would be compatible with a version of the myth in which Persephone or Hades himself chose to release Alcestis from the underworld because of her loving sacrifice. On the other hand, the pointed claim that Alcestis' choice made his father and mother "seem to be strangers in blood" (*allotrious*) to their own son and "in name only related" (*onomati monon*) seems to come directly from Admetus' renunciation of any ties of blood or devotion to Pheres (lines 666–8).

When or how Euripides' *Alcestis* was first performed again after its original staging in 438 is unknown. All surviving Greek tragedies were originally written with a single performance in mind, at one of the festivals honoring Dionysus. After the death of Aeschylus, the Athenian state decided to allow his plays to be restaged at later festivals, though just how this was arranged remains unclear. Euripides at the end of his life, like Aeschylus before him, traveled away from Athens to mount at least one of his plays at the court of a king in Thessaly. During his lifetime also some of his plays were produced during festivals at the deme theater of the Peiraeus, the harbor town for Athens.

Whether Euripides even contemplated the possibility of later re-performance when he was composing his plays, these works proved very popular with succeeding generations, continuing not only to be read (as they certainly were already in his lifetime)[3] but performed by the traveling companies of the Hellenistic and Roman age. Details of a specific performance of a specific play in antiquity after its initial production are remarkably rare, but there is a little more evidence in the case of the *Alcestis* than for most. Dramas performed by the Greek traveling players were more likely to inspire later poets and playwrights to take up the same theme. The Roman tragedian Accius, working in the late second to early first century BC, wrote a Latin *Alcestis*, undoubtedly motivated by Euripides' version. Precisely one line survives from this play, but in that line someone tells how Alcestis "shrieked" as she was dragged back from the underworld.[4] This small fragment suggests that Accius' Alcestis resisted giving up the fate she had embraced on behalf of her husband.[5] Her story held the stage for at least two more centuries, as the poet Juvenal shows, writing early in the second century AD. His *Sixth Satire*, an infamous diatribe against women, tells how "our wives watch Alcestis taking on the fate of her husband" (6. 652–3), implicitly contrasting her virtue with the watching Roman wives' depravity. These spectators might be watching Accius' version on stage, but Juvenal's reference to Sophocles in the same poem suggests that a performance of Euripides' original Greek version is more likely.[6]

Employing one of the most fascinating pieces of evidence for performance to come down to us from antiquity, C. W. Marshall has shown that a fragment of papyrus (P. Oxy. 4546) from the late first century BC or early first century AD, written in Egypt, was a working text for an actor rehearsing to play Admetus in a production of Euripides' text.[7] The fates have been very generous in preserving this evidence for us. While Alcestis' story is certainly represented in the visual arts, to which we will soon turn, the frequency of her story there is not in itself sufficient proof that Euripides' play held the stage throughout antiquity. Yet here in this papyrus fragment is precious evidence that, four centuries after her debut in Athens, her play was being performed for an audience of the Greek-speaking elite who still administered and profited from the richest realm conquered by Alexander, the kingdom and later Roman province of Egypt. If the *Alcestis* could command an audience in Egypt, it seems even more likely that the play was in the repertoire of performance at other major population centers in the Greek east.

In the late Hellenistic and Roman periods, enthusiasts and scholars begin to assemble collections of mythology. Some details of the accounts of Apollodorus (1.9.15 and 3.10.4) and Hyginus (51, 52) have been discussed above in Chapter 1.[8] These writers often choose to synthesize stories that once may have been quite separate, and one must bear in mind the potential for these syntheses to affect later versions, including both the performing and visual traditions. As allegorical interpretation of traditional myths gains ground in both the philosophical and religious traditions, the myths can be reshaped even more. We shall return below to one such allegorizing version from the late fifth century AD, attributed to Fulgentius.

An important aspect of the afterlife of *Alcestis* in the ancient world appears in funerary art and inscriptions. The chorus' wish in the second stasimon, "May the earth fall lightly upon you, lady" (463–4), is the first recorded example of an image that forms a staple of both Greek and Latin epitaphs, both real and imaginary.[9] So Meleager says in a literary version (*Palatine Anthology* 7. 461):

> Hail Earth, mother of all! Before now I, who was Aesigene, never weighed heavily on you, so now may you lie lightly over me.
> (trans. R. Lattimore)

The topos became familiar enough to be played with, as when Archaias, also in the *Palatine Anthology* (7. 204) asks that the dust lie heavily on a pet bird killed by a cat—lest the cat dig it up again!

The example of Alcestis is invoked in a number of funerary inscriptions, both actual and possibly literary. In another epigram from the *Palatine Anthology* (7. 791) the deceased claims "I am a new Alcestis, and I died on behalf of a noble husband," while surviving stone inscriptions as widely scattered as in Sardinia and Bulgaria compare the deceased to Alcestis.[10] Even Admetus seems still to be a model worth citing, as a pair of first-century AD inscriptions honoring a contemporary individual named Admetus shows.[11] For all of these later audiences, the story of Alcestis is unambiguously one of devotion and virtue.[12]

Alcestis' story and image appear on a number of Roman sarcophagi and tomb paintings, always as an image of marital fidelity and often of hope for a life after death. The durability of stone has made the sarcophagi the richer and more readable source. The sarcophagus of C. Junius Euhodus and Metilia Acte, found in Ostia and now housed at the Vatican, dates to the second century AD, perhaps a few decades after the wives in Juvenal attended that stage performance.[13]

Figure 1. Sarcophagus of C. Junius Euhodus and Metilia Acte, second century AD. Rome, Vatican Museum, Galleria Chiaramonti, I 3. Inv no. 1195.

The front of the sarcophagus depicts two scenes: Alcestis' death occupies the center, while including onlookers and other elements of the story to the left; Heracles conducting her from the underworld to Admetus forms the right-hand scene. Perhaps most startling for modern viewers is the fact that this is one of the earliest funerary monuments to incorporate the particular deceased it honors into the mythological narrative it depicts. The central figures of the dying Alcestis and Admetus bear older portrait visages representing Junius Euhodus and Metilia Acte. Admetus receiving the veiled woman at the right has Euhodus' features as well, though the woman there seems an idealized youthful figure.

While the dying Alcestis appears on a number of other sarcophagi, the scene of her return on this example offers the greatest interest. The scene telescopes both time and space in combining features of Euripides' version with other mythic variants. At the far right of the scene sits Hades enthroned, with Persephone at his side. Some other sarcophagi of the myth show Alcestis before the ruler of the underworld, but here she has already turned away, while Heracles, grasping her right hand as well as that of Admetus, prepares to unite the two in a gesture strongly reminiscent of non-mythic Roman wedding scenes on other sarcophagi.

Between Heracles and Admetus, a small Cerberus pokes his heads out of a cave-like opening. The role of Heracles and the motif of remarriage show the continuing influence of Euripides' vision on how Alcestis' story was imagined. An inscription demonstrates that the deceased couple were devotees of the cult of the Magna Mater (Great Mother goddess); they clearly hoped their marriage might last beyond the grave.

A sarcophagus lid now preserved in the Palazzo Rinuccini in Florence trims the story down to its even more essential elements.[14] The figures on the right show the wedding of Admetus and Alcestis, but he looks away from her, over his shoulder, and toward a scene on the left half where Heracles and Hermes lead the veiled Alcestis forth from the underworld. Marriage and remarriage stand thus side by side, linked by the figure of Admetus.

Alcestis is still there two centuries later, poised between the pagan and the Christian worlds. An inscribed fourth-century AD tomb painting shows how she can function as a guide and companion for the deceased in the underworld.[15] This work in the tomb of Vincentius and Vibia in a catacomb on the Appian Way shows Alcestis, clearly denoted in an inscription, joining Mercury in leading the deceased Vibia before the underworld judges, here named Dispater and Aeracura. This allows us to identify an earlier painting, probably second-century AD, from the Tomb of the Nasones on the Via Flaminia as the same motif. Though unlabeled and now known only through drawings, it depicts a very similar scene of Mercury and a veiled woman, almost certainly Alcestis, as he leads the deceased before her judges.

Alcestis' story could clearly resonate with the new adherents of Christianity. In the fourth-century AD catacomb of the Via Latina, scenes of Alcestis' story appear on the walls of cubiculum N, while Christian scriptural scenes appear in the very next chamber (and elsewhere in the catacomb). A novel scene in this treatment of her story shows a male figure on a sickbed, with a woman at his side and other lamenting attendants: this seems to be a stricken Admetus, at the moment Alcestis offers to take his place. Beverly Berg suggests that the patroness who ordered the tomb commissioned this scene to evoke her devotion to the husband who predeceased her.[16] Other paintings depict Heracles (unmistakable with club and lion skin) triumphing over a fallen opponent, probably Death. Elsewhere Heracles leads a veiled Alcestis from a cave opening, past Cerberus, and to a seated Admetus.

Figure 2. Alcestis beside Hercules and Ceberus, fourth century AD. Fresco in the Christian Catacomb of the Via Latina

Whether the couple laid to rest in this part of the catacomb were still adherents of the pagan traditions or Christians using classical themes, Alcestis' story evidently spoke to their devotion and their hopes for what might come next.

From Late Antiquity to the Renaissance

A late version of Alcestis' story in Latin hexameters survives on papyrus leaves now in Barcelona.[17] Initial assessments after its discovery have considered it to be an experiment in miniature epic, mostly consisting of speeches with a minimum of narrative connecting them, although Edith Hall has more recently suggested that it might be remnants of a libretto for a Latin pantomime.[18] In its 124 lines, Admetus asks Apollo to reveal his fate, and then, at the shocking news of his impending fate and possible escape, turns first to his father, then his mother. Both reject him, the father (like Euripides' Pheres) on the grounds that nothing is sweeter to him than his own life, while the mother urges the Stoic view that his own death is his debt to nature. Alcestis, called only "the daughter of Pelias" in the poem, volunteers in his stead, and our text ends as she cries out that Death is overtaking her.[19] A number of features seem owed directly to Euripides' play, notably Alcestis' request that Admetus not set a stepmother over their children and the fact that she prepares her own body for the funeral rites. Within the world of this poem, that means cremation, and she also imagines Admetus holding the urn with her ashes in his lap and honoring it. While highly rhetorical, the poem has considerable literary merit. There is no clear evidence, however, that this poem was known to the later Middle Ages.

Just how knowledge of the myth survived in the West after direct knowledge of Greek texts was lost is an interesting question. Probably the *Mythologiae* of the fifth-century Christian writer Fulgentius, which allegorically interpreted a number of myths including that of Alcestis (1. 22), was the principal source, supplemented by the earlier account of Hyginus (50–1). Boccaccio used Fulgentius in composing his *Genealogy of the Pagan Gods*, which also relates the story allegorically (13. 1) as a marriage of mind (Admetus) and courage (Alcestis).[20] One or more of these is presumably the source on which Chaucer drew for a number of poems.

Alcestis seems to have fascinated Chaucer. Characters in *The Canterbury Tales* mention her as though she should be familiar to an audience. Thus the introduction to the Man of Law's Tale (75–6) invokes her virtue as a wife along with Hypermestra and Penelope, and the Franklin's Tale (734–6) again links Alcestis with Penelope as one for whom "al Grece knoweth of hire chastitee." Chaucer relates her story more fully in book five of his *Troilus and Cressida* (section 219, lines 1527–33):

> As wel thow myghtest lien on Alceste,
> That was of creatures, but men lye,
> That euere weren, kyndest and the beste,
> ffor whan hire housbonde was in iupertye
> To dye hym self but if she wolde dye,
> She ches for hym to dye and gon to helle,
> And starf anon as vs the bokes telle.

> As well tell lies about Alceste
> who was of creatures (unless men lie)
> the kindest there ever was, and the best.
> For when her husband was in jeopardy
> of death, unless she would accept to die,
> she chose to die for him and go to hell,
> and die she did, as us the books tell.

Most significantly, Queen Alceste and King Admetus are the rulers in his unfinished *Legend of Good Women*. When the prologue tells her story here, it includes the detail that Hercules rescued her from hell and brought her "again to bliss."[21] Moreover, Chaucer uniquely imagines that Alcestis is then to be metamorphosed into the daisy, the symbol of love but also a prefiguration of Christ's redemption of the dead.[22]

Chaucer's contemporary, John Gower includes a very brief version of their story in his enormous *Confessio Amantis*. In Book VII he illustrates a point thus (1912–22):

> A womman is the mannes bote,
> His lif, his deth, his wo, his wel;
> And this thing mai be schewed wel,

> Hou that wommen ben goode and kinde,   1915
> For in ensample this I finde.
> Whan that the duk Ametus lay
> Sek in his bedd, that every day
> Men waiten whan he scholde deie,
> Alceste his wif goth forto preie,   1920
> As sche which wolde thonk deserve,
> With Sacrifice unto Minerve ...

His Alceste prays to Minerva for her husband and is granted the opportunity to take his disease upon herself. She gladly does—and dies—but there is no resurrection in Gower's version of the story.

From Shakespeare to the Nineteenth Century

> *Past ruin'd Ilion Helen lives,*
> *Alcestis rises from the shades;*
> *Verse calls them forth; 'tis verse that gives*
> *Immortal youth to mortal maids.*
>
> Walter Savage Landor

In Shakespeare's *The Winter's Tale*, the death of Queen Hermione and her eventual resurrection, first as a statue, then as a living woman, has suggested to more than one reader or viewer a resonance with the story of Alcestis. Shakespeare's immediate source for his late play was undoubtedly a prose romance, *Pandosto*, published by Robert Greene in 1588. Greene's work shows no direct influence from Euripides but also differs in a number of points from Shakespeare's version, including the suicide of the king rather than his eventual reconciliation with the queen. At least three Latin translations of the *Alcestis*, one of them intended for performance in schools, preceded the composition of *The Winter's Tale*, so it just possible that one of these or another, unknown intermediary influenced Shakespeare's redemptive vision of the virtuous wife returned from the dead to her remorseful husband.[23]

Alcestis certainly walks again in Milton's moving Sonnet 23, which begins:

> Methought I saw my late espoused Saint
>   Brought to me like *Alcestis* from the grave,
>   Whom *Jove's* great Son to her glad Husband gave,
>   Rescu'd from death by force though pale and faint.
> Mine as whom washt from spot of child-bed taint
>   Purification in the old Law did save,
>   And such, as yet once more I trust to have
>   Full sight of her in Heaven without restraint …

The allusion to Heracles ("*Jove's* great Son") shows that, unlike Shakespeare, Milton undoubtedly had the story direct from Euripides. Critical discussion has tended to worry about which of Milton's first two wives is the subject of the poem or the force of the allusion to his blindness in the final two lines.[24] For the classically inclined, however, there is great interest in observing how in the final sestet this embodiment of devotion and virtue turns into Creusa:

> Came vested all in white, pure as her mind;
>   Her face was veil'd, yet to my fancied sight
>   Love, sweetness, goodness, in her person shin'd
> So clear, as in no face with more delight.
>   But, O, as to embrace me she inclin'd,
>   I wak'd, she fled, and day brought back my night.

Although to be precise, Milton's Saint reaches to embrace him, rather than he her, the final lines surely invoke classical topoi of the living grasping for the shades of the dead. The closest model seems to be Aeneas, searching for his lost wife Creusa in the burning ruins of Troy. When her shade appears to him, Creusa commends their son to his loving care in language ("preserve now the love of our shared son," *nati serva communis amorem*, *Aeneid* 2. 789) that recalls both Propertius' Cornelia and Alcestis herself.[25] Aeneas tries to embrace her, but fails, and she vanishes like a dream (2. 792–4).[26] In waking from his dream Milton turns from Alcestis, the hopeful Greek adumbration of resurrection, to Creusa, the Roman embodiment of irredeemable loss—for she is the wife Aeneas will never see again, even in the underworld. The sonnet moves from future hope to present despair, from a Christian heaven to a classical hell. The turn suggests a darkness more visible than heretofore seen.

The story of Alcestis forms the subject of more than one opera in the seventeenth and eighteenth centuries, including Lully's *Alceste ou le triomphe d'Hercule*, the first French opera under the patronage of Louis XIV.[27] As time progresses, however, elements of the action begin to be suppressed or rewritten. The angry quarrel between Admetus and Pheres is regularly omitted, and often the confrontation between Apollo and Death. The writers become more embarrassed by the figure of Admetus and devise ever more complicated turns of the plot to explain how he could possibly have accepted his wife's offer to die in his place (often by having her make a binding pledge to the gods before he even finds out what she wishes to do).[28]

When Gluck first mounted his *Alceste* in Vienna in 1767, its Italian libretto (by Calzabigi) eliminated the role of Heracles in order to emphasize Apollo's gratitude.[29] Alcestis offers her own life for Admetus', unbeknown to her husband, and it is the god who chooses to restore her. When Gluck premiered the French version in Paris in 1776, its libretto originally also lacked Heracles, but in the face of less than enthusiastic audience reception, Heracles was restored to the plot in subsequent performances, although Apollo still made the final determination of her fate.[30]

The great tragedian Racine felt himself obliged to take up the defense of Euripides as a dramatist in the preface to his own version of *Iphigenia*, and fascinatingly, he chose the *Alcestis* as the means of doing so. He cites the "marvelous scene" in which the dying Alcestis sees the Ferryman coming for her and then accuses unnamed "contemporary writers" of disparaging and showing contempt for Euripides because they have so completely misunderstood the scene. He blames this in part on a bad edition of Euripides that misattributed these lines to Admetus and made *him* seem to be the one who feared his own death here. Racine may or may not be quite fair to his rivals here,[31] but the quarrel shows that some were already beginning to think of the story as one that showed the cowardice of Admetus just as much as it praised the courage (if not the sense) of Alcestis. While a self-sacrificing Alcestis, as much in love with death and glory as she is with her husband, could still suit well the sentiments of early Romanticism, she became much less at home as the nineteenth century rolled on. After Mary Wollstonecraft wrote *The Vindication of the Rights of Women*, could Alcestis ever seem as heroic as she once had?

Vittorio Alfieri's *Second Alcestis*, completed in 1799, shows the last stage of the baroque reworking of the legend and points forward to other developments. Alfieri presents his work as the translation of a rediscovered second version of Alcestis' story by Euripides (taking his cue from the known historical fact that Euripides produced two versions of *Hippolytus* in Athens).[32] When Act I opens, Pheres is a kind father, desperately worried over his son's illness. Alcestis announces Apollo's oracle from Delphi that Admetus will be cured—but then reveals she has already agreed to take her husband's place, news she shares with her healed husband in Act II. Act III begins with her farewell to household and children, Act IV with the arrival of Hercules, who finds Admetus nearly lifeless with despair and Alcestis comatose. Hercules orders that Alcestis be taken to the temple of Mercury and Apollo. Just before departing, he revives Admetus, but when the latter goes to look at Alcestis' body one final time, it has disappeared from the temple. Admetus announces that he will starve himself to death. In the last act Hercules returns with the veiled woman, offering her as a new wife, whom Admetus rejects. Hercules reveals her true identity, Alcestis herself reassures her husband that heaven reunites them, and the play ends with general rejoicing. Alfieri thus employs all the recent strategies intended to evoke sympathy for both husband and wife, remaking Pheres into a loving and selfless father in the bargain, but he also hints that Alcestis has not really died, only traveled to the very point of death, from which Hercules somehow brings her back.[33] In this Alfieri adopts a strategy similar to that already used in antiquity by the rationalizing Greek writer Palaephatus (perhaps as early as the fourth century BC), who explained the miracles of myth in "scientific" ways. In his *Incredible Tales* 40, Palaephatus explains Alcestis' resurrection as a "cure" by a physician—named Heracles.[34]

Euripides' own text seems not to have been much revived until the latter half of the nineteenth century, although in England earlier burlesque versions (including musical parody) were popular and may have contributed to interest in Euripides' original. For the Strand theater in London Frank Talfourd wrote and produced *Alcestis or The Original Strong-Minded Woman* in 1850 with himself in the title role, and the script was revived several times thereafter.[35] Talfourd himself labeled his version "a shameless misinterpretation of the Greek drama of Euripides," and his Alcestis has little but contempt for her Admetus, "weak in intellect," who has run up debts to Orcus/Death that he cannot meet. Henry Spicer's 1855 *Alcestis* was a more serious affair, a "lyrical play" using Gluck's music; his heroine offers herself after she fails to find another substitute for her husband's life. Its operatic staging included scene changes and "lurid" lighting effects for the confrontation of Heracles and Orcus, which Hall and Macintosh suggest influenced Frederic Lord Leighton's magnificent painting *Hercules Wrestling with Death for the Body of Alcestis* (c. 1869–71: fig. 3 and cover illustration).[36]

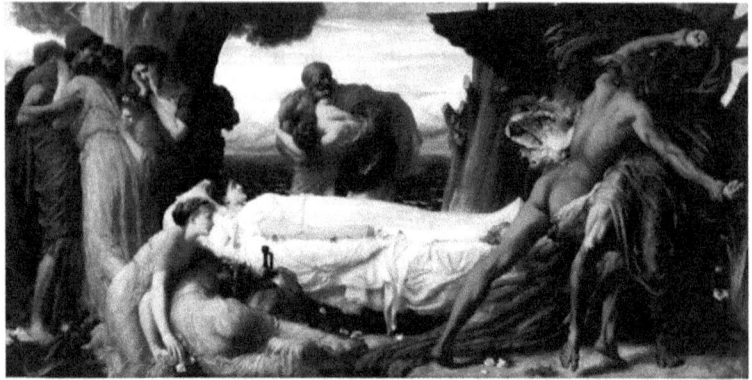

Figure 3. Frederic Leighton, *Hercules Wrestling with Death for the Body of Alcestis*, 1869-71. Oil on canvas. Wadsworth Atheneum, Hartford, Connecticut, USA.

School performances in Greek included an *Alcestis* at Reading in 1809, although we know that the director, Dr Richard Valpy, eliminated Pheres from the 1824 performance as "a bad moral example."[37] Bradfield College in England began its tradition of Greek plays with an *Alcestis* in 1882.[38] In 1887 the Oxford University Dramatic Society wanted to stage the *Alcestis* but were prohibited by university regulations from allowing a male undergraduate to play any female roles. They were able to recruit the already well-known Cambridge classicist, Jane Harrison, in Oxford to give a course of lectures on Greek art, to play the title role—to excellent reviews from the Oxford classicists, and less sympathetic ones from the popular press.[39] In America, Beloit College, which had begun its Greek play tradition in 1885, mounted its first *Alcestis* in 1889.[40]

Classical scholarship played an important role in changing perceptions of the *Alcestis*, although it took some years for effects to be widely felt. In 1834 the German scholar Dindorf published his edition of the play and included the summary now termed the second hypothesis (ancient notes on the play, preserved in a Vatican manuscript). Only this source preserves the information that the *Alcestis* was performed in 438 BC, along with three other plays of Euripides—and that it was the last play in that group. Dindorf's edition thus revealed for the first time to the world in general that the *Alcestis* filled the slot normally occupied by the satyr play. After the publication of the Vatican manuscript, the genre of the play and its seriousness were suddenly open to question; it had become a problem play, and for most scholars has remained so to this day.

The poets were less easily swayed—or more generous than the scholars. In 1871 Robert Browning published a remarkable version of the *Alcestis* in the form of his poem, "Balaustion's Adventure: including a Transcript from Euripides."[41] Some 2,700 lines long, the poem is framed as a dramatic monologue by Balaustion, a Rhodian woman whose name means "wild pomegranate flower."[42] For a group of female listeners (addressed in lines 3–4 and elsewhere), she recalls earlier events of her life, beginning with her attempt during the Peloponnesian War to flee with her family from the spreading strife. Cast up on Sicily, as Athenian sympathizers they are at first threatened by the Syracusans—until their captors discover that Balaustion knows great amounts of Euripides, including the *Alcestis*, which she partly recites, partly narrates to enthusiastic throngs. The frame story, including their eventual escape to Athens, occupies over 300 lines at the beginning of the monologue. Then the narrator begins such a mixed recital and narrative of the play for her internal audience. Browning affixed to this poem an epigraph of lines in praise of Euripides from the work of his own late wife, Elizabeth Barrett Browning, and at least one scholar has therefore seen in the female narrator Balaustion a reanimation of Elizabeth Barrett Browning.[43]

Browning's method combines translation with often forceful interpretation. We hear Apollo and Death speak, but Balaustion offers interpretive commentary as well (e.g. 429: "Till Death shrilled, hard and quick, in spite and fear"). The reader sees Browning wrestling for psychological plausibility at points where the Greek text seems most alien. Balaustion first conjectures that Death's sword has already "cut the soul at once / from life" (677–8) when the dying Alcestis speaks in a "hard dry ... monotone" and then goes on to point out to her hearers (695–6):

> For, you shall note, she uttered no one word
> Of love more to her husband, though he wept ...

Browning includes apparent interjections from Balaustion's audience in this scene as well but indicates that they—and we readers—must wait for more before judging.[44]

Browning sees the self-interest of Admetus, but sees much more as well. Thus the grieving husband's descent into "low strife" with his father reveals their essential similarity (1364–9):

> Like hates like:
> Accordingly Admetos,—full i' the face
> Of Pheres, his true father, outward shape
> And inward fashion, body matching soul,—
> Saw just himself when years should do their work
> And reinforce the selfishness inside ...

Yet Browning's Admetus is capable of learning, as Balaustion's comment after their scene shows (1590–3):

> So, the old selfish Pheres went his way,
> Case-hardened as he came; and left the youth,
> (Only half-selfish now, since sensitive)
> To go on learning by a light the more ...

In many ways, the poem's real hero is Heracles, larger than life in every way and operating both as mortal and hero in the narrated play action and in the frame story, for Balaustion calls upon him to save her in the frame story, and it is on the steps of his temple in Syracuse that she gives her first performance of Alcestis' story. Her narrative mocks the servant who dares to condemn Heracles for roistering when others mourn, showing that the servant was as complicit in Alcestis' death as was Admetus. Only Heracles can rescue the whole household and restore the wife to a "renovated" husband (2327–34):

> It was the crowning grace of that great heart,
> To keep back joy: procrastinate the truth
> Until the wife, who had made proof and found
> The husband wanting, might essay once more,
> Hear, see, and feel him renovated now—
> Able to do, now, all herself had done,
> Risen to the height of her: so, hand in hand,
> The two might go together, live and die.

The poem closes with the narrator's meditations on other possible versions of Alcestis' story, how "You, I, or anyone might mould a new / Admetos, new Alkestis" (2415–16). Much is remarkable in how Browning re-envisions the narrative, but nothing is so striking as his use of a female narrator and a female internal audience to critique but also ultimately to understand the human actions.

By century's end the brilliantly polemical Greek scholar A. W. Verrall, by contrast, found in Browning's version an irresistible target, which he often cites. In his 1895 book *Euripides the Rationalist*, Verrall concluded that Euripides' plays were deeply ironic and regularly demonstrated the opposite of what their surface meaning seemed to be. The *Alcestis* is his leading example, for not only is Admetus in his view a thoroughgoing coward, but the play's miraculous ending is a delusion in which he and others are complicit: "The purpose of the *Alcestis* as a whole … is … to expose [the legend] as fundamentally untrue and immoral."[45] Alcestis, deceived by those around her into believing that her last hour is at hand as well as exhausted with lamentation and self-starvation, simply lapses into unconsciousness. Her callous husband hustles her off to the burial ground as soon as possible. Heracles finds her waking from her swoon but tacitly conspires with Admetus to conceal the fact that he has done nothing whatever heroic to rescue her. All the characters are thus deluded or venal and the concluding miracle a complete fraud.

While very few would accept Verrall's overall interpretation today, its legacy lingers. Alcestis herself can now seem surprisingly unsympathetic (a trait Browning seems to be the first to acknowledge, even as he argues against it), focused on her own fame and lacking any word of tenderness for the husband she has chosen to die for. The great Greek scholar Gilbert Murray edited the standard Oxford text of Euripides in the early twentieth century but also wrote widely known and appreciated translations, some of which were professionally staged on both sides of the Atlantic.[46] Murray was in fact the model for the Greek professor, Adolphus Cusins, in G. B. Shaw's remarkable *Major Barbara*. The well-known Shakespearean actor (and later producer) Harley Granville Barker played Cusins in the original production and was even made up to look like Murray.[47] Murray's *Alcestis* translation, first published in 1915, was not among those staged in the West End, though it shares many stylistic features with those that were. T. S. Eliot in a famous essay attacked the Swinburnian verse of Murray's Euripides,[48] but more than poetic imagery was at issue. In particular, Murray inserted various endearments into Alcestis' speeches to her husband that simply do not exist in the Greek—an attempt, whether conscious or unconscious, to accommodate her character to a role more psychologically acceptable to the contemporary audience.[49]

The Twentieth Century

One of the major verse dramas of the twentieth century draws inspiration from Euripides' *Alcestis*—though no one noticed this until the author himself pointed it out. When T. S. Eliot won the Nobel Prize for Literature in 1948, he was already at work on *The Cocktail*

Party, first produced at the Edinburgh Festival in 1949.[50] Only in his Spencer Lecture on "Poetry and Drama" at Harvard in 1950 did Eliot gleefully reveal:

> [N]o one of my acquaintance (and no dramatic critics) recognised the source of my story in the *Alcestis* of Euripides. In fact, I have had to go into detailed explanation to convince them[51]

Despite Eliot's own testimony, the critics have taken some convincing. Those who do acknowledge Euripides' influence, like those of his friends Eliot goes on to mention, have been most willing to see the disruptive but then redemptive figure of Heracles behind the difficult and mysterious guest at the party in Eliot's Act I, who is unknown to his reluctant host Edward but seems to know so much about his situation and the wife who has then left him, Lavinia.[52] This unknown guest proves later to be the psychiatrist whom Lavinia has already consulted and whom Edward is manipulated into seeing professionally by other friends and guests at the party. The play's portrait of a marriage that has died, yet can be resurrected by the intervention of others, translates some, if by no means the whole, of the Alcestis story for its contemporary audience—and does so with considerably greater moral complexity than many present readings of Euripides' play. Edward's self-centered approach to life, including the affair he is engaged in, clearly reveals his inadequacies as a husband, but the wife who leaves him and then returns, Lavinia, undergoes a moral growth along with his.[53] In a fascinating variation on Euripides' dichotomy between the heroic and self-sacrificing Alcestis of the play's first part (and the chorus' heroine worship) and the returned wife, faced with the equally difficult task of living again, Eliot divides these roles between two characters, Lavinia the returned wife and Celia, Edward's one-time mistress who chooses instead a life of service to others—a life which ends, we learn somewhat awkwardly at the party in the second act, in gruesome martyrdom while serving as medical missionary.

The Alcestiad

Another major writer was drawn to the Alcestis theme at about the same time. Thornton Wilder began work in 1939 on the play that was eventually published under the title, *The Alcestiad*.[54] He took a draft of part of the play off with him when he joined the Air Force in World War II, but those papers were lost, and he had to begin again. In 1954, after his success with *The Matchmaker*, Wilder was invited to offer another play to the Edinburgh Festival, and he chose to return to his Alcestis theme. Directed by Tyrone Guthrie and starring Irene Worth as Alcestis and Robert Hardy as Admetus, a three-act version of his play was produced for the 1955 festival. Public reception was good, critical reception mixed, and Wilder allowed no further performances for a time. He then added a satyr play entitled "The Drunken Sisters" (separately published in 1957) and shaped the whole into *The Alcestiad*. An offer from the Schauspielhaus in Zurich led to a translation into German and several productions in Germany as well as Vienna and then an operatic version, composed by Louise Talma. The first American production came only in 1978, at the Pacific Conservatory for the Performing Arts, three years after Wilder's death.

The Alcestiad incorporates material and motifs not only from parts of the legend omitted by Euripides but from other tragedies as well. Act I begins with a confrontation of Death and Apollo, but we soon discover that this is not the day of Alcestis' death, but her wedding day—and Alcestis is far from sure that she wishes to marry at all. She confides to her servant that she always wanted rather to be a priestess of Apollo but now is to marry Admetus because he passed her father's test. A comic interlude with Teiresias intervenes; the old prophet cannot quite remember whose palace he has come to or what prophecy he is to deliver, but he introduces four herdsmen, one of whom—though no one can tell which one—is Apollo in human guise. Alcestis hopes for a message from this hidden Apollo but receives none. Informed of her hesitation by her servant, Admetus generously offers to release Alcestis from their impending wedding, but nonetheless declares his enduring love for her. Moved, Alcestis prompts him to ask her for her hand again, and the act ends with her free promise to marry him.

Act II opens 12 years later. Admetus is dying, having been stabbed accidentally by one of the four herdsmen in a drunken brawl. A written message arrives from Delphi: it proclaims that Admetus will not die—if someone else wishes to die in his place. Though the herdsman offers his own life, Alcestis insists that only she can make this sacrifice and withdraws. Admetus emerges into the light, staged much as the dying Alcestis herself is in Euripides' play. Alcestis returns, clad in her wedding dress from Act I, and as they talk, his pains and weaknesses gradually disappear as she takes them on. Admetus does not notice the change at first, and even when Alcestis says that she would find it natural to die for him, if such a message came from Delphi, he can confidently but obviously reply: "No. No. No man would wish another to die for him. Every man is ready to die his own death." Only after he has said "I would think less of the gods who could lay such a decision between husband and wife"[55] does he notice Alcestis is collapsing. As she is carried off, he follows, and Hercules arrives. Admetus returns, at first concealing her death, but eventually confessing it to an appalled and then angered Hercules, who in very short order descends to the underworld through a cave represented below the palace and then silently brings her veiled figure back back to Admetus, who takes her into the palace.

Act III offers the most unusual treatment. It is again twelve years later. Admetus and two of his children are dead, the third has disappeared, and an aged Alcestis creeps about the palace. A new and unrelated king rules the palace, while plague afflicts the land. The king and his followers blame Alcestis for bringing the plague by returning from the dead, though the populace at large is still sympathetic to her. Apollo confronts Death again, and Death blames him both for taking Alcestis away and for sending all the new plague victims to the underworld. The missing son, named Epimenes in Wilder's version, returns in disguise with a companion in a motif obviously modeled on Orestes and Pylades in Aeschylus' *Oresteia*. By falsely reporting Epimenes' death they hope to get close enough to the usurping King Agis to assassinate him, but first they tell the tale to an unrecognized Alcestis. She recognizes her son, tries to dissuade him from the murder, and even stands between King Agis and her son. While Epimenes assumes command of the townspeople and goes off to organize relief from the plague, Agis' daughter, Laodamia, dies of the plague, and his will to continue is broken. Alcestis is left alone onstage except for Apollo. In a motif surely borrowed from Sophocles' *Œdipus at Colonus*, he leads her away through the place gate to his sacred grove, and the main play ends.

Apollo returns for a brief transitional scene, lectures the audience on satyr play, dons a slave's disguise, and then as the curtain rises on the three Fates at work, he joins in "The Drunken Sisters." Performing the traditional comic role of the running slave, he pretends to be carrying special wine for Aphrodite which is the secret source of her beauty. The Fates seize the wine from him, quickly become inebriated, and are tricked into a riddle contest with the disguised Apollo, which he naturally wins. He claims the life thread of Admetus as his prize—but learns to his horror, as the curtain falls, that this will only work if someone agrees to die in his place; he recognizes too late that this will be Alcestis.

Following strategies familiar since the seventeenth century, Wilder incorporates more and more into the play to bolster both Admetus' claim to be someone worth dying for as well as Alcestis' role as one motivated by love rather than compulsion. Pheres is banished from the play altogether, and the boisterous Hercules (who startlingly reveals that he loves Alcestis so devotedly because she forgave him after he once attempted to assault her!) is given fairly short shrift as well, as both first and second acts concentrate on developing the love of husband and wife for each other. The curious third act makes Alcestis at once Electra and the anti-Clytemnestra: she is the abandoned relict of the fallen royal house, but she refuses to allow her son to kill the usurper. She justifies her protection of King Agis in this speech to her son Epimenes:

> A man who has known the joys of revenge may never know any other joy. That is the voice of your father.[56]

Despite the sufferings of her house and her people, Apollo enshrines her at the end as a heroized *daimon*, watching over her people. The sparse production history of the play in the English-speaking world suggests that Wilder's case has not proved particularly compelling, but it remains an intriguing experiment.[57]

Ted Hughes' *Alcestis*

The most recent adaptation of the *Alcestis* is the posthumously published version by Ted Hughes.[58] While the main lines of the play are those of Euripides, Hughes has markedly expanded certain portions and interpolated other material.[59] The result, as Hallie Marshall has recently argued, weds the Euripidean narrative to a much more symbolist approach to drama.[60]

Apollo's four-page opening speech (expanding 27 lines in Euripides) both narrates more of and rewrites the background story. He equivocates over his own status ("You may call me a god. / You may call me whatever you like")[61] and claims Zeus is ultimately responsible for everything. After he persuaded the Fates to allow the exchange and Admetus' parents refused, Apollo himself took over the quest for a substitute:

> I was shameless. I asked everybody …
> Only one person I did not ask:
> Alcestis. His wife.
>
> But now you know her story. Of her own accord
> She has volunteered—to give him her life.[62]

Hughes thus employs the now-familiar strategy of making Alcestis volunteer without Admetus asking her. In an almost metatheatrical touch, chorus members on their arrival discuss whether this is really so:

> Chorus 2
>
> If you ask me, Admetos is a strange one
> To let her die in his place.
>
> Chorus 3
>
> Once she'd agreed I thought it was too late
> For him to do anything about it?
>
> Chorus 1
>
> Better not look at it too closely.[63]

Admetus' speech to the dying Alcestis forcefully rejects the kind of memorialization Euripides' Admetus imagines:

> I swear this before the gods.
> Alcestis, everything has gone with you.
> What shall I do,
> Have some sculptor make a model of you?
> Stretch out with it, one our bed,
> Call it Alcestis, whisper to it?
> Tell it all I would have told you?
> Embrace it—horrible!—stroke it!

Knowing it can never be you.
Horrible! ...[64]

This leads Admetus into an extended passage on the story of Orpheus and his attempt to rescue his dead wife. Hughes had avoided the story of Orpheus before, perhaps because of the potentially painful biographical resonances with the death of his own wife, the poet Sylvia Plath,[65] but here he allows Admetus to dwell on it, only to conclude with Orpheus' failure and the same word that resounds through the previous passage on the imagined sculpture: "Horrible!"

Hughes' Heracles is accompanied by two followers, named Lichas and Iolaus, who in his drunken revelry help him playfully re-enact his labors with the aid of other servants. Heracles begins to have visions of the underworld, with his own dead wife there. Iolaus tells him:

Iolaus

You had a strange nightmare.
A horrifying dream. Your dream became famous.
You told it and they made a play about it.
You're getting your dream mixed up with what will happen.
You're thinking of that play.

Heracles

What was the play?
The madness of Heracles. Was that the title?[66]

"That play" is clearly Euripides' *Heracles*, the story of the hero's madness and slaughter of his own family, events lying in the future for the characters of this *Alcestis* (as they did also in Euripides' version). The sequence culminates in a vision of Prometheus chained to his mountain and tormented by a vulture. Both Prometheus and the vulture have speaking parts. With an arrow from his bow Heracles shoots the vulture, which bursts into flame and falls (according to

Hughes' stage directions), then frees Prometheus—although he then must shoot the vulture a few more times.

Prometheus vanishes with his mountaintop, and the play returns to its more Euripidean lines. The servant apprises Heracles of the death of Alcestis, and he leaves to rescue her: "Every labor so far has served / Only to prepare me for this."[67] Admetus returns, mourns with the chorus, and Heracles returns with the veiled woman. His persuasion of Admetus is much briefer than in Euripides, but his endorsement of his host's values much more explicit: "Take her to your chambers. And in future / Honour your guests."[68] The version as a whole offers a sympathetic portrayal of Admetus and ends, as one review put it, "on a triumphant note with the late Poet Laureate's message to us from the edge of the grave … 'See how God has accomplished / What was beyond belief. / Let this give man hope.'"[69]

Chronology

c. 534 BC:	establishment of the City Dionysia festival at Athens, victory of Thespis as tragic poet
c. 525:	birth of Aeschylus
c. 507:	reforms of Cleisthenes; establishment of democracy at Athens
c. 499:	Aeschylus' first production
c. 495:	birth of Sophocles
490:	defeat of the first Persian invasion of Greece at Marathon
486:	establishment of competition for comic poets at the City Dionysia
484:	Aeschylus' first dramatic victory
481–479:	second Persian invasion, defeated at Salamis (480) and Platea (479)
480–475:	birth of Euripides
472:	Aeschylus wins first prize with tetralogy containing *Persians*
468:	Sophocles' first dramatic victory
462:	reforms of Ephialtes; extension of democracy at Athens
458:	Aeschylus wins first prize with *Oresteia* tetralogy
456/5:	death of Aeschylus
455:	Euripides competes for the first time, places third with tetralogy including *Daughters of Pelias* (*Life of Euripides* 15, 32)
451/0:	enactment of Pericles' citizenship law
449:	establishment of competition for tragic actors at the City Dionysia
441:	Euripides' first dramatic victory, titles unknown

438:	Euripides wins second prize with *Cretan Women, Alcmaeon in Psophis, Telephus,* and *Alcestis* (Sophocles places first)
431:	Euripides wins third prize with *Medea, Philoctetes, Dictys,* and *Theristai* (satyr play)
431:	beginning of the Peloponnesian War between Athens and Sparta
428:	Euripides wins first prize with *Hippolytus* (second version)
415:	Athenian expedition against Sicily sails (defeated 413)
415:	Euripides wins second prize with *Trojan Women, Alexander, Palamedes,* and *Sisyphus* (satyr play)
412:	Euripides produces *Helen* and *Andromeda* (placement not known)
408:	Euripides produces *Orestes*
407/6:	death of Euripides in Macedon
406/5:	death of Sophocles
after 406:	Euripides' *Bacchae, Iphigenia at Aulis,* and *Alcmaeon in Corinth* win first prize in posthumous production by his son
405:	Aristophanes' *Frogs* depicts Euripides and Aeschylus competing for the throne of tragedy in the underworld
86:	Death of Accius, author of a Roman tragedy entitled *Alcestis*
1st cen. BC/ 1st cen. AD:	actor's rehearsal script for *Alcestis* (P. Oxy. 4546) written in Egypt
c. 110 AD:	Juvenal's *Satire* 6. 652–3 mentions performance of *Alcestis* at Rome
5th cen. AD:	Fulgentius' *Genealogy of the Pagan Gods* allegorizes Alcestis' story

Chronology

c. 1375–95:	Chaucer's *Canterbury Tales*, *Troilus and Cressida*, and *Legend of Good Women* all mention Alcestis
c. 1390:	Gower's *Confessio Amantis*
c. 1652–8:	Milton's Sonnet 23
1799:	Vittorio Alfieri's *Second Alcestis*
1871:	Robert Browning's poetic monologue "Balaustion's Adventure: including a Transcript from Euripides"
1895:	A. W. Verrall publishes *Euripides the Rationalist*
1915:	Gilbert Murray's translation of *Alcestis*
1949:	premiere of T. S. Eliot's *Cocktail Party*
1955:	Thornton Wilder's *A Place in the Sun* (early version of the *Alcestiad*) produced at Edinburgh Festival
1999:	posthumous publication of Ted Hughes' *Alcestis*

Abbreviations

FGrHist	F. Jacoby, *Fragments of the Greek Historians* (Berlin: Weidmann, 1923).
IG	Deutsche Akademie der Wissenschaften zu Berlin, *Inscriptiones Gracae, consilio et auctoritate Academiae Litterarum Borussicae editae* (Berlin: G. de Gruyter, 1924–).
LIMC	*Lexicon Iconographicum Mythologiae Classicae* (Zürich: Artemis, 1981–).
Meiggs and Lewis	R. Meiggs and D. M. Lewis, *A Selection of Greek Historical Inscriptions to the End of the Fifth Century B.C.* (Oxford: Clarendon Press, 1969).
PCG	R. Kassel and C. Austin (eds), *Poetae Comici Graeci* (Berlin: W. de Gruyter, 1983–).

Glossary

agôn. In Greek culture generally, a "contest"; in tragedy, a pair of successive monologues by two characters debating central issues of the play, followed by dialogue.

aidôs. A complex emotion or set of attitudes including a sense of respect, modesty, reverence, and shame.

anapaests. A slower meter, consisting of a short and two long syllables (⏑⏑−), sometimes considered a marching rhythm.

anceps. In meter, a syllable that can either be short or long (indicated by x).

antistrophe. See **strophe**, below.

charis. Grace, kindness in the abstract, but also a gracious gift or favor.

choregos. A wealthy citizen assigned the duty at the festival of paying for training the chorus and outfitting the production, roughly the producer today.

chorus. In Euripides' time, fifteen singer/dancers who performed in the orchestra and represented a group within the fiction of the play.

dactylic meter. A more excited meter, consisting of a long and two short syllables (−⏑⏑).

deme. A smaller political unit of the Athenian city-state, a village.

demos. The citizenry, the body of adult male citizens considered collectively.

Dionysia. Any religious festival in honor of Dionysus, god of wine and theatre. The City Dionysia took place in late March, according to our calendar.

eccyclêma. A wheeled platform, which could be rolled out of the *skênê* building to reveal a scene set in the interior.

eisodos, pl. **eisodoi.** See **parodos**, pl. **parodoi.**

episode. A scene of the drama, consisting primarily or solely of performance by the actors, separated from the next episode by a **stasimon** (q.v.) sung by the chorus.

exodos. Song sung by the chorus during their exit at the end of the play.

hypothesis. An ancient summary of information about a play, including plot and production details, preserved in some later manuscripts.

iambic trimeter. The meter used to approximate ordinary speech in Greek drama, with a line consisting of three pairs of short and long syllables (x-⏑-/ x-⏑-/ x-⏑-); see also **anceps** and **resolution**.

orchêstra. The "dancing place"—i.e., the open space in front of the *skênê* where the chorus sang and danced.

parodos, pl. parodoi. The entranceway on either side, leading to the orchestra and stage building of the theatre; sometimes called **eisodos**.

parôdos. Song sung by the chorus during their entry into the **orchestra**.

resolution. Replacement of one metrical element, usually a long syllable, by two short syllables.

satyr play. The fourth play of a tragic **tetralogy**, characterized by its chorus of satyrs (part-man, part-beast, with horse tails, snub noses, and pointed ears), with some other characters drawn from mythology but more freely invented plots.

scholion (pl. **scholia**). An ancient scholar's (**scholiast's**) annotation to a literary text, usually preserved in the margins of a later manuscript.

skênê. The stage building with at least one doorway onto a platform in front. The *skênê* could represent any building or enclosed space required by the fiction of the play.

stasimon. Song sung by the chorus within the play, separating the **episodes** (q.v.).

strophe. A unit of choral verse, followed by a metrically identical unit of verse called the **antistrophe**.

tetralogy. Four plays (three tragedies and normally a satyr play) composed by a tragic poet for the competition at the City **Dionysia**.

Guide to Further Reading

This guide singles out the principal texts, commentaries, and translations easily available in English, as well as some general works on Greek tragedy and a selection of studies of the *Alcestis*. The following Bibliography includes all the works of secondary scholarship cited in the footnotes.

Note that texts and commentaries are cited in the notes by author's last name alone. Where commentaries are keyed to line numbers in the Greek text, the abbreviation *ad* means "commentary at line number" (*ad loc.*, if the line number has been previously noted).

Texts, Commentaries, and Concordance

D. J. Conacher (ed.), *Euripides: Alcestis* (Warminster: Aris & Phillips, 1988).
A. M. Dale (ed.), *Euripides: Alcestis* (Oxford: Oxford University Press, 1954).
J. Diggle (ed.), *Euripidis Fabulae* (Oxford: Oxford University Press, 1981–94). The standard Greek text of Euripides in three volumes: *Alcestis* is in volume one.
C. Luschnig and H. Roisman (eds), *Euripides' Alcestis* (Norman: University of Oklahoma Press, 2003), with extensive commentary and Greek vocabulary.
M. McDonald, *A Semilemmatized Concordance to Euripides' Alcestis* (Costa Mesa, CA: TLG Publications, 1977).
L. P. E. Parker, *Euripides: Alcestis* (Oxford: Oxford University Press, 2007), with introduction and commentary.
G. Seeck (ed.), *Euripides: Alkestis* (Berlin and New York: Walter de Gruyter, 2008), with translation (German) and commentary.

Translations

W. Arrowsmith, *Euripides: Alcestis* (New York: Oxford University Press, 1974).

R. Blondell, M.-K. Gamel, N. S. Rabinowitz, and B. Zweig (eds), *Women on the Edge: Four Plays by Euripides. Alcestis, Medea, Helen, Iphigenia at Aulis* (New York and London: Routledge, 1999).

J. Davie, *Alcestis and Other Plays* (London: Penguin Books, 1996).

D. Kovacs (ed.), *Euripides: Cyclops, Alcestis, Medea* (Cambridge, MA: Harvard University Press, 1994).

R. Lattimore (ed.), *Euripides I: Alcestis, Medea, Heracleidae, Hippolytus* (Chicago: University of Chicago Press, 1955).

G. Murray, *The Alcestis of Euripides* (London: G. Allen & Unwin Ltd., 1915; New York: Oxford University Press, 1915).

R. Waterfield, *Alcestis, Heracles, Children of Heracles, Cyclops* (Oxford: Oxford University Press, 2003).

Adaptations

Robert Browning, "Balaustion's Adventure: including a Transcript from Euripides," pp. 867–942 in *Robert Browning: The Poems*, ed. J. Pettigrew, vol. 1 (New Haven: Yale University Press, 1981).

T. S. Eliot, *The Cocktail Party: A Comedy* (London: Faber & Faber, 1950; New York: Harcourt Brace and Co., 1950).

T. Hughes, *Euripides' Alcestis in a New Version by Ted Hughes* (London: Faber, 1999; New York: Farrar, Straus and Giroux, 1999).

Thornton Wilder, *The Alcestiad, or A Life in the Sun, with a Satyr Play, The Drunken Sisters* (New York: Harper and Row, 1977).

General Studies of Greek Tragedy and Reception

D. Carter (ed.), *Why Athens? A Reappraisal of Tragic Politics*. (Oxford: Oxford University Press, 2011).

E. Csapo and W. J. Slater (eds), *The Context of Ancient Drama* (Ann Arbor: University of Michigan Press, 1995). Translations of major ancient sources on Greek and Roman drama, with commentary and illustrations.

P. E. Easterling (ed.), *The Cambridge Companion to Greek Tragedy* (Cambridge: Cambridge University Press, 1997).

J. R. Green, *Theatre in Ancient Greek Society* (London: Routledge, 1994). A study of drama's place in Greek society, drawing on material evidence (architecture, vase-painting, terracottas, mosaics, sculpture, etc.).

J. Gregory (ed.), *A Companion to Greek Tragedy* (Malden, MA and Oxford: Blackwell, 2005).

E. Hall and F. Macintosh, *Greek Tragedy and the British Theatre, 1660–1914* (Oxford and New York: Oxford University Press, 2005).

A. W. Pickard-Cambridge, *The Dramatic Festivals of Athens*, 2nd edn, revised by J. Gould and D. M. Lewis (Oxford: Oxford University Press, 1968). The fundamental study of the evidence for Athenian dramatic festivals. Greek is not translated, though many texts are translated by Csapo and Slater (above); not easy going for beginners.

R. Scodel, *An Introduction to Greek Tragedy* (New York: Cambridge University Press, 2010).

A. Sommerstein, *Greek Drama and Dramatists* (London and New York: Routledge, 2002).

O. Taplin, *Greek Tragedy in Action* (Berkeley, CA: University of California Press, 1978).

B. Zimmermann, *Greek Tragedy: An Introduction*, trans. Thomas Marier (Baltimore, MD: The Johns Hopkins University Press, 1991).

Books and Articles on *Alcestis*

E. M. Bradley, "Admetus and the Triumph of Failure in Euripides' *Alcestis*," *Ramus* 9 (1980): 112–27.

A. P. Burnett, *Catastrophe Survived*, Ch. 2, "*Alcestis*" (Oxford: Oxford University Press, 1971).

R. G. A. Buxton, "Euripides' *Alkestis*: Five Aspects of an Interpretation," pp. 170–86 in *Euripides*, ed. J. Mossman, *Oxford Readings in Classical Studies* (Oxford: Oxford University Press, 2003) [= pp. 17–31 in L. Rodley (ed.), *Papers Given at a Colloquium in Honour of R. P. Winnington Ingram* (London, 1987)].

V. Castellani, "Notes on the Structure of Euripides' *Alcestis*," *American Journal of Philology* 100 (1979): 487–96.

M. Dubischar, "Euripides, Alkestis 1970–2000," *Lustrum* 47 (2005): 55–80 (with a "Bibliographisches Addendum, Euripides 2001–2005," pp. 711–12 on *Alcestis*). A comprehensive listing of secondary scholarship on the *Alcestis* for these 35 years, with comments on these works in German.

M. Lloyd, "Euripides' *Alcestis*," *Greece & Rome* 32 (1985): 119–31.

F. Macintosh, "Alcestis in Britain," pp. 281–308 in M.-H. Garelli-François, P. Sauzeau, and M.-P. Noël (eds), *D'un "genre" à l'autre* (Cahiers du GITA, 14; Montpellier, 2001).

S. L. Schein, "ΦΙΛΙΑ in Euripides' *Alcestis*," *Metis* 3 (1988): 179–206.

C. Segal, "Euripides' *Alcestis*: Female Death and Male Tears," *Classical Antiquity* 11 (1992), pp. 142–58 (expanded version in Segal 1993—see below).

G. Smith, "The *Alcestis* of Euripides: An Interpretation," *Rivista di Filologia e di Istruzione Classica* 111 (1983): 129–45.

M. Stieber, "Statuary in Euripides' *Alcestis*," *Arion* 5 (1997–8): 69–97.

J. E. Thorburn, "The Third Stasimon of Euripides' *Alcestis*," *Scripta Classica Israelica* 19 (2000): 35–49.

S. Wood, "Alcestis on Roman Sarcophagi," *American Journal of Archaeology* 82 (1978): 499–510.

Notes

Chapter 1

1 The second Hypothesis states *Alcestis* was "seventeenth" among Euripides' plays. The likeliest explanation is that some plays from four previous tetralogies had already been lost when the numbered list was compiled.
2 Recorded on the Parian Marble A60. It is just possible that we have a record of that victory, the inscribed stone base for a bronze statue honoring a choregos or producer of an unnamed Euripides play. The inscription (*IG* I3 969) names the choregos, Socrates, a general in the Samian War of 441/0, Euripides as didaskalos of the chorus, and fourteen chorus members. It does not name the play or even the festival, but on balance it seems more likely to have been a monument erected in his home deme by the victorious choregos from the city competition; see Wilson 2000, 130–6.
3 Pickard-Cambridge 1988, 84–5.
4 See Csapo and Slater 1995, 105–8 for a recent discussion of the problems of festival chronology.
5 On the tetralogy see Dale 1954, v-vii; on *Telephus*, Webster 1967, 44–8, Heath 1987. The fragments of *Telephus* are available with commentary, facing translation, and a very helpful introduction by M. J. Cropp in Collard, Cropp, and Lee 1995, 17–52.
6 On the festival and its ideology see Goldhill 1990, supplemented by Goldhill 2000.
7 Details of the structure and order of events that comprised the City Dionysia remain problematic; see Pickard-Cambridge 1988, 65–8 for what is still the likeliest account. Parke 1977, 132 dates the Proagon to the 9th of Elapheboleion for reasons I cannot determine. During the Peloponnesian War the festival program may have been shortened by one day (against this view see Luppe 1972 and Luppe 2000, with other references), but in 438 it still had its original form. It seems at least one

day intervened between the Proagon and the first tragic entries, which spread over three days.

8   Socrates describes Agathon at the Proagon for his tragedy as "being about to reveal your *logoi*" (Plato, *Symposium* 194b); cf. Pickard-Cambridge 1988, 67.

9   No ancient source describes a play rehearsal in detail. Pollux 4, 106 and Phrynichus the Atticist, *Sophistike Proparaskeue*, mention the *choregion* as a place where the chorus or the chorus and actors together were rehearsed, but both of these sources are much later than our plays. In the best discussion of rehearsals and location, Davidson 2003, 112–14 briefly speculates that there might have been scruples about conducting all rehearsals at the theater in the sanctuary itself, but he reasonably concludes that at least one final rehearsal must have taken place there. Cf. also Wilson 2000, 71–4, 81–6.

10 Marshall 2000.

11 Sometime in the fourth century BC but before 341, the program was changed, and a single satyr play was performed before the rest of the festival: Hall 1998, 19 and n. 15; Pickard-Cambridge 1988, 79.

12 Aeschylus' plays were re-performed in the fifth century at Athenian dramatic festivals, but only after his death. It may already have been possible to see some plays re-performed at the Rural Dionysia in the fifth century, but there was no regularity to this, and only a fraction of the audience will have had such an experience.

13 Hesiod frr. 122–7. A scholion to *Alc.* 1 says that Euripides is following the Hesiodic account in his play and refers also to other, now lost, possible sources including Asclepiades, Stesichorus, and Pherecydes, but we have no direct evidence.

14 The marriage and Alcestis' sacrifice: Apollodorus 1.9.15. Apollo's enslavement to Admetus: Apollodorus 3. 10. 3–4; cf. Zenobius, *Cent.* 1. 18. See also the second-century Latin account, the *Genealogies* or *Fables* attributed to Hyginus (51, 52), with only Heracles as rescuer.

15 Murray 1915, ix assumes it; cf. Gauly 1991, 42–5; 661 and the tenuous inferences in Conacher 1988, 31. Snell *TrGF* 69–73 gives the full testimonia, but none of these suggests Phrynichus' *Alcestis* was a satyr play. Cf. Slater 2006.

16 *ad* Verg. *Aen.* 4. 694. Phrynichus was famous for his lyrics, which apparently survived in symposia and elsewhere as separate songs. It is possible that the detail of the sword was embedded in such a song, but an actual visual memory of the original production seems the more likely source.
17 Plutarch, *Them.* 5 quotes an inscription to show that Themistocles was choregos for this production.
18 *Suda* f 762.
19 Several scholars have recently argued for a much smaller capacity, in the range of 4,000 to 7,000 spectators, confined to the area on which the wooden benches were erected: see the discussion in Csapo 2007, 97–100, with further references. Even at these much lower numbers, the attendance would have exceeded that at most sessions of the democratic assembly.
20 Winkler 1990, 39 and n. 58; Henderson 1991.
21 On the crane see Mastronarde 1990.
22 The actor of Admetus can in principle play either Apollo or Death in the opening scene. A fascinating papyrus surviving from the Roman period seems to suggest it was a text of just the lines for an actor playing the part of Admetus. It is fragmentary, missing both beginning and ending: maddeningly, the number of lines per column in the text is consistent with this actor having played either Apollo or Death in the missing first portion of the papyrus. The brilliant study of Marshall 2004 suggests the doubling of Admetus with Death for this late production was more likely. See further Chapter 4, 70, below.
23 For the most recent study of voting procedure, see Marshall and van Willigenburg 2004.
24 Callipides in 418 BC.
25 It can be shown with some degree of certainty that Creon is the through-line in Sophocles' *Antigone*, the character to which all others react. Does this make him the hero of the play? Perhaps not—but his role is a good guide to how Sophocles structured his play.
26 Wohl 1998, 150 (who apparently meant to write "two speaking actors" rather than three) suggests the audience would be aware at the end of this play that the actor playing Heracles had earlier played Alcestis,

thus silencing Alcestis and replacing her "tragic" speech with his "sympotic singing."

27 Bassi 1989, 20, although see also Slater 1997, 101–2 and Slater 2002, 301n. 84 and 314n. 18.

Chapter 2

1. For a discussion and defense of the stage direction, recorded in the scholia, that Apollo enters from the house of Admetus, see Buxton 2003, 170–1.
2. Some visual identification seems necessary, since Apollo does not name himself, and the myth may not be instantly recognizable by the audience. Luschnig and Roisman (2003, 50) suggest Apollo may be dressed as a hunter (to go with the bow) or perhaps still as a herdsman, implying that he is only at this very moment ceasing his period of service in the house of Admetus.
3. Whether this implicitly confirms or denies the version from other legend that Apollo made the Fates drunk is an open question; Kilpatrick (1986, 6) suggests the latter.
4. While both younger and older versions of Thanatos appear when he is paired with his brother Hypnos (Shapiro 1993, 132–48), in the rare depictions of Thanatos alone he is regularly older and bearded (Shapiro 1993, 159–65).
5. The reference to "black-winged Death" at line 843 depends on the acceptance of a likely emendation to the text there. Though wingless versions of Death appear in vase painting, the winged iconography is far more common (Shapiro 1993, 132–48).
6. On the iconography of Death, see Jan Bazant, s.v. Thanatos, *LIMC* VII, 1, 904–8. The lekythos is Paris Louvre CA 1264 (ARV2 1384, 19: Group R); also Shapiro 1993, 164, fig. 109.
7. It is amusing, and instructive for later reception of the play, to compare two nineteenth-century versions of Death in the play. Verrall (1895, 100) imagines Apollo and Death together as "two well-bred landlords … discuss[ing] a question of encroachment." For him Death is no

"King of Terrors," just a "punctilious usurer," in contrast to Robert Browning's imagination of Death as "some dread heapy blackness." For further comparison of the views of professor and poet, see Chapter 4, 83–6, below.

8 Dale *ad* 77–135; Luschnig and Roisman 2003, 68.
9 Rosenmeyer 1963, 222; Bell 1980, 55 n. 8; O'Higgins 1993, 81.
10 Translators regularly supply an object for the verb "betray" in this line, but there is none in the Greek; in context, it more likely means "betray herself, give up her will to live" (Seeck *ad* 202).
11 Dale *ad* 238–43 (so also Conacher, Seeck *ad* 233). Luschnig and Roisman (2003, 92–3) argue for the *eccyclêma*. If the vocal exertion demanded by Alcestis' song was greater than that required for trimeter dialogue, the actor may have remained standing throughout this section, despite the dramatic implausibility from a modern point of view, and only sunk to the couch after line 272.
12 Rosenmeyer (1963, 226) thinks that a mute figure playing Charon appeared—though if so, why not Hades too? Leaving both to the audience's imagination is far preferable.
13 Iakov (2010, 20) attempts to reconcile the two statements, suggesting that Alcestis' request is that Admetus not remarry before the children have come of age, noting that Penelope claims Odysseus made a similar request of her, should he not return from Troy, that she not remarry until Telemachus was of age (Homer, *Od.* 18. 269–70). Whether the audience would puzzle out this loophole for Admetus during performance is another question.
14 The suicide of the title character in Sophocles' *Ajax* raises other problems, and we must infer the action from the text. Given the difficulties of staging, it seems most likely that the actor playing Ajax disappears behind bushes or some type of scenery for his suicide, allowing a mannequin to be revealed thereafter as Ajax's corpse. The actor is needed to play other roles and cannot be left lying onstage for the rest of the performance.
15 See Sifakis 1979, 67–80, esp. 69–70, as well as Parker 2007, 131–2.
16 O'Higgins (1993, 82) points to the parallel in language of Pindar, *Nemean* 8, 11–12.

17 The chorus does *not* point out, though the audience may well remember, that Apollo was condemned to this service by Zeus (Seeck *ad* 570).
18 See Thorburn 2000 on the tone and effect of this stasimon as a whole and especially 41–2 on Apollo as an Orpheus or Pan figure, 46 on the use of anthropomorphizing vocabulary for the animals' response to his music.
19 I follow the punctuation of Dale 1954 and others. Diggle 1981, Conacher 1988, and Parker 2007 punctuate differently, so that the line would mean roughly: "All things are possible for honorable men; I am in awe of (their? his?) wisdom."
20 Lattimore 1955: "for this godly man, the end will be good." Conacher 1988: "all will go well for a god-fearing man." Rabinowitz (Blondell 1999, 125) preserves the structure: "a god-fearing man will do well." No one, however, seems to bring out the force of *kedna*.
21 See LSJ s.v. for other meanings and connotations, all positive. The chorus describes Alcestis herself as a "dear wife" (*kednês … gunaikos*) at 97.
22 Parker (2007, 199–201 *ad* 746) is almost alone in doubting that the chorus departs here and gives a detailed discussion of the textual signals or lack thereof for chorus movement.
23 Garner (1988, 65), comparing Hector imagining a future traveler passing the tomb of his fallen opponent. As Parker (2007 *ad* 1003) notes, *makaira daimon* indicates "that Alcestis will be a 'hero,' in the technical, religious sense."
24 The Greek text of the play does not explicitly refer to a veil, but it may be inferred from Admetus' failure to recognize her immediately and his explicit conclusion that she must be young based on her garb and appearance (*esthêti kai kosmôi*, 1050; cf. the scholiast's comment: *ên gar perikekallumenê*). The author of the Hypothesis attributed to Dicearchus suggests that Heracles veiled her: *esthêti kaluptei tên gunaika*. See the discussion in Mignanego 2003 and Lush 2012, 397–8 and n. 24.
25 Montiglio (2000, 187) details how carefully the audience's attention is drawn to the gesture. Admetus' marked reference in his lament to

holding Alcestis' hand in their wedding procession at 917 may look forward to this moment. On the hand gesture as symbolizing marriage, Lush 2012, 400–1, with further references. Later representations, especially on sarcophagi, juxtapose their original wedding and the return of Alcestis to Admetus; see Wood 1978, 509, with further discussion in Chapter 4, 71–3, below.

26 Some in the audience of *Alcestis* might remember the ghost of Darius in Aeschylus' *Persians*, produced nearly 50 years before, and Euripides himself would later raise the ghost of Polydorus in his *Hecuba*. For Segal (1993, 50), Admetus' final expression of fear here is one last look "into the empty mirror of tragedy" before the play achieves its final romantic or comic ending.

27 Wohl (1998, 151) offers the intriguingly metatheatrical suggestion that "The three days of her silence correspond to the three days of tragic performance at the City Dionysia: when she will be able to speak again, the tragic festival will be over." Because Alcestis does not speak here, it is possible for this play, like Euripides' *Medea*, still to be performed only by two actors—yet Euripides need not have called explicit attention to her silence. Euripides certainly had three actors available in 438; reconstructions of the *Telephus*, performed with *Alcestis*, strongly indicate three-actor scenes: see Rehm 1994, 196 n. 48 and Heath 1987. Betts (1965) offers one religious explanation but, even more importantly, notes that Heracles does *not* say that Alcestis *cannot* speak but rather that it is not proper (*themis*) for Admetus to *hear* her speaking.

28 *Andromache*, *Helen*, and *Bacchae*. The last four of the verses seem to conclude his *Medea*, just seven years later. Scholars tend to think these final lines belong best to *Alcestis*, but see also Luschnig and Roisman 2003, 160–1.

Chapter 3

1 Schlegel as quoted by Woolsey 1853, iii. Schlegel in fact saw in Euripides' work as a whole a sharp decline from the tragic worldview

of Aeschylus and Sophocles and is prepared to criticize Admetus' "selfish" interest in living, but his praise of Alcestis is unmixed. On Schlegel's views and influence, see Parker 2007, xl–xli.

2 Notable examples are by P. Peyron (1794, Raleigh) and F. H. Füger (1804–5, Academy, Vienna); see also the discussion of Frederic Leighton's version in Chapter 4, below.

3 House (*domos*): 48 examples; home (*oikos*): 14 examples; home (*dôma*): 13 examples; halls (*melathra*): 6 examples (lines 23, 29, 77, 248, 567, and 862). In short, there is a reference to a house roughly once every 14 lines in this play.

4 On this ode see Thorburn 2000 and on the house esp. Luschnig 1990, 19–36.

5 Compare the form and tone of the very first line of Euripides' *Andromache* as the title character cries out to the lost "Form of Asia's land" (*Asiatidos gês schêma*, 1).

6 Burnett 1971, 43; cf. Luschnig 1990, 31–2.

7 Buxton 2003, 170–3. Note that Admetus attempts to keep Heracles "outside the doors" even when a guest in his palace: after he persuades Heracles to stay with him, Admetus instructs the servants to close the courtyard doors (*thuras metaulous*, 549) to protect the guest quarters from the sounds of mourning in the main house.

8 It is perhaps not immediately obvious whether the possessive phrase "of my Iolcian homeland" applies only to the "bridal chambers" or all three nouns in the series, but Dale (1954 *ad* 248–9) explains: "Turning now to Earth, Alcestis calls upon the palace of Pherae before her and the bridal chamber in her childhood's home in Iolcus ..." Elsewhere (177, 911ff.) the play presumes the actual marriage of Alcestis and Admetus took place here in Pherae, not in Iolcus. Whether a room in her father's palace in Iolcus could be called a bridal chamber (*numphidioi koitai* are in fact "bridal beds," though here presumably a metonym for the chamber) without the wedding having been consummated there is obscure, but it may be part of a "bride of Hades" theme in this scene. Just as Alcestis was a prospective bride as she left her father's halls in Iolcus, so now she is, as she leaves Admetus' house, the prospective bride of Death.

9   Rabinowitz (1999, 400n. 63) concludes that, in the mythic setting of the play, someone marrying a widowed Alcestis would, as the suitors of Penelope on Ithaca hoped to and as Œdipus at Thebes did, become king in place of the deceased ruler.
10 Well brought out by Luschnig 1990, 35–6.
11 Seaford 1994; Griffith 1995; cf. Murnaghan 1999, 109–10.
12 Apollodorus 1. 9. 15–16.
13 For example, Loraux 1987, 28–9; Segal 1992, esp. 152: "Through Admetus' prolonged display of grieving and weeping, Euripides explores the places where the rigid dichotomies of male and female behavior in this society collapse and where there is even an overlapping of male and female roles." Cf. Foley 1992, 140–1; Luschnig 1992, 13–14 and n. 6; and especially the suggestive remarks of Zeitlin 1990, 86–7 on how the tragic hero often "undergoes some species of 'feminine' experience."
14 Foley 1992, 142 and n. 43.
15 Rehm 1994, 90–1.
16 Women who die as human sacrifices also die in public, though offstage; cf. Loraux 1987, esp. 43–7. By contrast, the death of Aegisthus inside Agamemnon's palace in Aeschylus' *Libation Bearers* is another part of the feminization of his character.
17 Artemidorus, *Onirocritica* 4.30 and 2.49; Rosenmeyer (1963, 246–7) calls attention to these passages as well. In the literate age of the Second Sophistic, Artemidorus concludes the list of physical signs at 2.49 with "and written lists of property," not part of the oral and mythic milieu of the *Alcestis*.
18 Eumelus was also one of the suitors of Helen who later married Iphthime, sister of Penelope, and was one of the warriors inside the Trojan horse at the fall of the city (Apollodorus 3. 10. 8; Homer *Od.* 4. 797; Quintus Smyrnaeus 12. 324). On Perimele see Hesiod fr. 194a Most, 256 Merkelbach West [= Antonius Liberalis 23]; Hyginus *Fabulae* 21.
19 Cf. Wohl 1998, 132–8 on Alcestis' displacement of Admetus as "patriarch" of the house.
20 Luschnig 1992, 25.

21 On *gêrotrophia* see Rubinstein 1993 *passim*. Thury (1988, 203) sees Admetus redefining the notion of the family here.
22 Scodel (1979, 58) connects this to *philia*, noting that "Admetus' parents have failed the test" of *philia*, with the result that (61) "[i]n this play, blood ties are divorced from *philia*. Wife and guest-friend are *philoi*, but the father cast away not only any desire for *arete* and *kleos*, but *philia*." On Pheres and *philia*, cf. Burnett 1965, 248.
23 Loraux 1986, 23: "Thus the lists of the dead mention neither patronymic nor demotic: freed forever from the bonds to father or family, the warrior was in effect entrusted with an official mission"; cf. Bradeen 1969, 147, 149. As Mark Toher has pointed out to me (pers. comm.), citing Clairmont 1983, 234–9, there are later casualty lists from the Peloponnesos (two each from Tegea and Mantinea, one from Argos) with names arranged by tribe. A tribal organization for the army may be broader than a solely Athenian development, even though the Athenians associated their tribes with Cleisthenes, the pioneering reformer who shaped the classical democracy. It is the absence of the patronymic in Athenian lists, rather than the presence of the tribal one, which is the significant point.
24 See for example Gregory 1991, 35–6 and n. 47, who compares Socrates' professed shock at Euthyphro's prosecution of his father (*Euth.* 4a).
25 Translation from Perseus (Dent, Everyman, 1910). Sicking (1998, 50–4) offers insightful discussion of this passage and the Athenian context for interpreting the Admetus-Pheres scene.
26 A key point of Stanton 1990 for this play. On parallels between marriage itself and *xenia*, see Rehm 1994, 93–4.
27 Konstan (1997, 33–7) offers a succinct and penetrating account, though he is skeptical about the heritability of obligation. On the role of *xenia* in creating networks among ruling families such as the rulers in myth, see Griffith 1995, 68–72 and *passim*.
28 See Belfiore 2000, 157 on Diomedes as a contrast to the good host, Admetus. Diomedes' horses were mares, like all chariot horses (Dale 1954 *ad* 486), and later rationalizing views (Σ Aristophanes, *Eccl.* 1129 and Hesychius) explained them as Diomedes' daughters, whom he prostituted to travelers in order to lower their guard before killing

his visitors. It seems unlikely, though, that this interpretation was in circulation as early as the *Alcestis*.

29 Schein 1988 is a superb study of *philia* and its associations in this play. Much of this section is indebted to his work.

30 Many find the line difficult: see Dale 1954 *ad* 279, Rabinowitz 1999, 400n. 61. The Greek verb *sebomai* means "worship" when applied to the gods; it cannot quite mean that with *philia* as its object, but it implies a powerful sense of reverence or honor.

31 Compare Heracles' statement that loving the dead (*philêsai ton thanont'*, 1081) brings only tears.

32 On the theme of *charis*, see Padilla 2000, to whom much of the following is indebted.

33 Konstan (1997, 90) observes that both Admetus and Heracles behave here as Aristotle advises (*Nic. Ethics* 9. 11): offering each other aid but trying not to burden each other with private griefs.

34 Stanton 1990, 48.

35 There is some anxiety over the text here. Wilamovitz thought to delete lines 1093–4, Dale lines 1094–5 (see her comments *ad loc.*), while Murray retained all. Diggle (1981) would delete 1094–5 as well, but see Stanton 1990, 44n. 8.

36 See also Wohl 1998, 152–3 on the impossibility of exchanges in this play.

37 For example, in his *Acharnians* 396–7, where the servant of Euripides tells a caller at the door that his master "is within and not within." This confusion of life and death recurs in other Euripidean plays: cf. *Trojan Women* 1223 "you shall die, not dying," and *Ion* 1444 "having died and not died." Perhaps the most striking parallel, almost a self-parody, occurs in the late and also problematic *Helen*, where Teucer, answering Helen's question about her brothers, says (138) "They are dead and not dead; there are two stories (*logô*)."

38 Stieber 1998, 78–9.

39 Arrowsmith 1974, 25, with discussion.

40 This discussion draws heavily upon the work of Wright 1986, Suter 2003, and Suter 2008. A clear summary of Wright's criteria for identifying lament in tragedy, including criteria for differentiating full and reduced laments, appears in Suter 2003, 2–4.

41 Wright 1986, 113–15, 117–19, and 124–5; Suter 2008, 164–5, 172. Themes such as wishing the marriage had never taken place, expressed by both the son (412) and Admetus (880), are familiar topoi in lament (as noted by Wright) and not (*pace* Luschnig and Roisman 2003, 108) pointed comments at Admetus' expense.

42 Where Wright (1986) noted many variations on the "full" lament, Suter (2003, 2008) usefully terms all the others "reduced." Yet the full laments which close Sophocles' *Œdipus Tyrannus* (1307–66) and Euripides' *Suppliants* (1114–64) and *Andromache* (1173–1225) are all shorter than the reduced lament here.

43 Resolution in meter means the substitution of two short syllables for a single expected long syllable in the metrical pattern. On the expected metrical patterns in lament, see Wright 1986, 113–15.

44 Bassi 1989, 25.

45 Loraux 1987, esp. 7–30.

46 Compare the onstage death of the matriarch of the Barrymore-like acting clan at the end of Kaufman and Ferber's comedy *The Royal Family* (first produced in 1927).

47 Garner 1988, esp. 60, noting the praise of Alcestis' kindness to the humble; cf. Patroclus' treatment of Briseis, *Il.* 19. 295–300, and Hector's kindness to Helen, *Il.* 24. 767–75.

48 Vermeule 1979, 101–5.

49 Griffith 1995.

50 Goldhill 1990, 105.

51 See Gregory 1991, 6 and n. 18 for criticisms of the lack of nuance in Goldhill's view of the pre-play ceremonies. On the orphans' ceremony cf. also C. Meyer 1993, 56–8.

52 The city certainly did bestow one crown in the fifth century (if we accept a restoration in the text) in the theater: that awarded to Thrasybulus for his role in the assassination of Phrynichus (see *IG* i2 110 = Meiggs and Lewis 85).

53 *Against Ctesiphon* 41–42, trans. C. D. Adams:

> It frequently happened that at the performance of the tragedies in the city proclamations were made without authorization of the people, now that this or that man was crowned by his tribe, now that

others were crowned by the men of their deme, while other men by the voice of the herald manumitted their household slaves, and made all Hellas their witness; and, most invidious of all, certain men who had secured positions as agents of foreign states managed to have proclaimed that they were crowned—it might be by the people of Rhodes, or of Chios, or of some other state—in recognition of their merit and uprightness.

54 See Cole 1993, 29 on crowning at the festival. Note that we only know about the libations performed by the generals before the tragic performances precisely because of improvisation in the ceremony. Plutarch's *Life of Cimon* (8. 7–9) tells how the archon in 468 drafted the generals as the ten judges of the tragic competition, instead of appointing the ten judges from the tribes by lot as was usual. The temporary innovation suggests that the fifth-century Dionysia was still fluid and evolving in a way that may no longer have been true in the fourth century.

55 Alan Sommerstein's notes in his edition of *Birds ad loc.* are particularly helpful here; cf. Melanthius *FGrHist* 326 F 3. The earliest evidence we have for the proclamation of an honorific crown at the Dionysia is *IG* i3 102.12–14.

56 Aristophanes, *Thesmophoriazusae* 338–9.

57 Loraux 1986, 26–8 on the status of the orphans.

58 Lysias (*In Theoz.*, P. Hib. I. 14, Budé). Lysias claims that Theozotides is attacking "the most noble proclamation of those in the laws." See Slater 1993 for a suggestion that Theozotides may have been aiming at preventing abuse of the Athenian practice of posthumous adoption.

59 Loraux 1986; cf. Goldhill 1990, 109–13.

60 Thucydides does not even mention the casualty lists in his account of Pericles' *epitaphios* (Loraux 1986, 22). De-emphasizing the individual dead was part of the democratic ethos in the latter half of the fifth century, as attested by the apparent ban on sculpted stone funeral monuments (E. Meyer 1993 and below, "Alcestis' Statue").

61 Goldhill 1990, 112 and esp. n. 52, citing Socrates' speech at the end of the *Crito* 53b and ff. Cf. Patterson 1990, 61 on Pericles' words and law as "examples of the appropriation by the polis of the language of family inheritance and membership."

62 Luschnig 1990, 21: "When Alcestis hands the children over to Admetus, she uses words and gestures associated with adoption (375)." Luschnig and Roisman 2003, 106 *ad* 371–6 now speak of a "property transfer." Adoption in Greece was essentially a private contract between adopter and adoptee (Rubinstein 1993, 34–5). Presumably, adoption of a minor (actually quite unusual in the historical sources, although a passage in Menander, *Samia* 695–9, indicates Demeas adopted Moschion as a child) was then a contract between natural and adoptive fathers. The language between Alcestis and Admetus ("on these conditions, receive the children" "I receive them"; 375–6) does sound quite contractual.

63 On the formula *anêr agathos genomenos* and its variants, see Loraux 1986, 99–101.

64 Hartigan 1991, 23. Luschnig (1992, 17–18) suggests some reasons why mention of other members of Alcestis' and Admetus' more extended families is suppressed in the play. One of the best (and briefest) accounts of the scene between Admetus and Pheres is Lloyd (1992, 37–41), who, after a careful analysis of the "lucid" structure of the scene, concludes (41) that "[t]he agon in *Alcestis* … is first and foremost a debate about Pheres' refusal to sacrifice himself, and it deals only incidentally with Admetus' acceptance of Alcestis' sacrifice."

65 There are traditionally ten pairs, but lists vary. A starting place is Aristotle, *Metaphysics* 1, 986ab.

66 Dale 1954 *ad* 77–135. Euripides divides the parodos of his later *Trojan Women* between two half-choruses, but prior to the *Alcestis* our only possible examples are the chorus of Aeschylus' *Seven against Thebes*, which divides its loyalties at the play's end, and the chorus of Sophocles' *Ajax*, which mid-play divides to search east and west for the hero. The date of the *Ajax* is unknown, but 450–40 is often suggested, with late in that range favored, so it may have offered a near precedent for the *Alcestis*.

67 One reading of a difficult passage in the second hypothesis is "There are five choregoi." This cannot mean five chorus leaders but might mean five individual voices speaking; see Dale 1954 *ad* 77–135; Luschnig and Roisman 2003, 68.

68 Wilamowitz suggested Euripides was echoing a statue motif from his own *Protesilaus*, in which the widowed Laodameia kept an image of her deceased husband, the play's title character, in her bedroom (see Dale 1954 *ad* 348–54; Webster 1967, 86: the resemblance is the basis for Wilamowitz's dating of the *Protesilaus*, however).

69 Lucian *Erotes* 13. Compare also the stories reported in Athenaeus XIII 605 F, including one at Samos, for which he cites Alexis fr. 41 K.-A. (and see Arnott 1996 *ad loc.*).

70 Segal 1993, 37–50; on the *kolossos*, 38–9.

71 Vernant 1985, 325–38. Cf. the brief but careful remarks on the term *kolossos* in Donohue 1988, 26–7 and n. 65. Wax dolls could also be termed *kolossoi*; see the intriguing discussion of the use of *kolossoi* in sacred law in Cyrene in Schaefer 1957, 228.

72 The evidence consists primarily of the so-called "menhirs" found in Bronze Age Midea and a pair of stone statuettes from a "possible cenotaph" on seventh-century Thera; see Faraone 1992, 82–3; Kurtz and Boardman 1971, 178–9, 258–9, and fig. 34. By contrast there is ample evidence for the use of cenotaphs: see Garland 1985, 102, 165 (with references). The Spartans used an image or *eidolon* of their fallen king Leonidas to celebrate his funeral when his body could not be recovered (which Herodotus 6. 58 calls their "custom"; see Toher 1991). Since Herodotus knew this story in the 440s, it might well have been part of the cultural repertoire of the audience of *Alcestis*. If there is any distant allusion, however, note that Euripides has converted the public use of a male heroic image into the private use of a female one—a possibility that the play's ending must erase.

73 E. Meyer 1993, 108; see also n. 18. The notion of a legal ban is not universally accepted; for example, Morris (1992, 145–9 and *passim*) has argued that the decline in monuments is widespread at this period in the Greek world. At a minimum, an Athenian would be perfectly familiar with his own city's practice and would find Admetus' notion of statue of Alcestis not just strange on its own but a violation of Athenian norms, whether enforced legally or only socially. Cf. Humphreys 1993, 120–2 on the sharp change from archaic aristocratic practice to the more democratic fifth century.

74 Stieber (1998) offers a careful and insightful reading of the play's references to an already built tomb for Alcestis and other imagery of funerary statuary. Most improbable, however, is her notion that the Alcestis who appears at play's end is not an actor representing the character, but something representing the already carved, inanimate tomb sculpture of Alcestis that Heracles has brought back. The bizarre comedy of such an ending is incompatible both with the fifth-century audience's experience of funerary commemoration and the whole reception history of the play in antiquity.

75 Goldhill 1990, 124.

76 Buxton 2003, esp. 173–9; Rehm 1994, 84–96.

77 It is this parallelism that deprives the objection of Segal 1992, 148 ("Euripides could have let [Admetus] refuse the woman first and then have him rewarded for his new firmness and understanding") of its force.

78 The scene would be perfectly at home in one of the later Greek novels, where bridegroom and bride are hailed as perfectly matched for each other (e.g. Chariton, *Callirhoe* 1.1).

79 Faraone 1999, 80. I am most grateful to my colleague Sandra Blakely for bringing this study to my attention.

80 Belfiore 2000, 49–53; 53 (citing Pythogorean views in particular). By contrast Lush (2012, 401 n. 31) sees the handclasp as "a ritual reenactment of abduction." On the Greek wedding more generally, see Oakley and Sinos 1993.

81 Belfiore 2000, 52.

82 Bradley 1980, 112.

83 Arthur Conan Doyle, "Silver Blaze":

> "Is there any point to which you would wish to draw my attention?"
> "To the curious incident of the dog in the night-time."
> "The dog did nothing in the night-time."
> "That was the curious incident," remarked Sherlock Holmes.

84 See Montiglio 2000, 179 on this scene and more generally on veiling and speech (cf. Mignanego 2003, 53–4).

85 Admetus' word *anaudês* (speechless) can mean "incapable of articulate speech." He seems to assume that Alcestis would have spoken by now,

if she were capable of doing so—but Heracles' answer definitively turns this issue to the propriety of his hearing (*kluein*). Cf. Betts 1965 and Wohl 1998, 150.

86 In fact two writers of ancient comedy treated the story, although we cannot be certain that either portrayed conversation between the two after Alcestis' rescue. Antiphanes *Alcestis* fr. 30 K.-A. has someone (Admetus, Heracles, and a prologue have all been suggested) urging that new and different methods be tried. Aristomenes competed against Aristophanes' *Wealth* in 388 BC with an *Admetus* (see *PCG* test. 4b).

87 Shakespeare, *Coriolanus* II i 175.

88 Foley 1992, 150–1, citing Cavell 1981. Foley's overall point is to suggest that a deep structure of the Demeter-Kore myth underlies both *Alcestis* and *Helen*, which she terms "anodos dramas." While some structural similarities to the Kore myth are undeniable, they are at the more general level of the "bride of Hades" motif in treatments of death (Loraux 1987, 37–8 and n. 22 points out that the wedding to Hades is remarkably *absent* in fifth-century epitaphs of women); the myth does not seem to me to "explain" the joyous ending of *Alcestis* on its own. Castellani (1979) demonstrates ways in which this short play structurally is in fact two plays: a tragedy, followed by a comedy ending in a (re)marriage. Halleran (1982) notes how the rare use of double antilabe connects the two halves, more specifically the death of Alcestis to her "rebirth" in her remarriage to Admetus.

89 Foley 1992, 138–9; Buxton 2003, 173–6.

90 Sissa 1990, 55, citing Aristotle (*Politics* I 1260a30) citing Sophocles.

91 Lloyd 1985, 121.

Chapter Four

1 Carm. Conv. 14 PMG; alluded to in Aristophanes' *Wasps* 1239, *Pelagroi* fr. 444 K-A., and Cratinus fr. 254 K-A.

2 For a full discussion see Scodel 1979; more briefly, Dale 1954, xi.

3   In Aristophanes, *Frogs* 52–3, the god Dionysus mentions reading one of Euripides' plays, so they were certainly circulating in written form before the end of the fifth century.
4   "When she had shrieked, dragged back again from the underworld" (*cum striderat retracta rursus inferis*, fr. 20 Warmington). The fragments of early Latin tragedy are easily accessible in English only in the Loeb editions, *The Remains of Old Latin*.
5   See further Slater 2002a.
6   Marshall 2004, 38 and n. 49, which credits this suggestion to Susanna Braund.
7   Marshall 2004.
8   Pp. 8–9; compare also Zenobius, *Cent.* 1. 18 for the story of Apollo's servitude to Admetus.
9   The following section relies on Lattimore 1962, 65–74. He cites simple versions of the theme from inscriptions at Rhodes in the first century BC (*IG* 12. 1. 151, 3–4) and Crete in the first century AD (*EG* 195. 1).
10 Sardinia: *IG* XIV 607, first/second century AD; Odessos, Bulgaria: *IGBR* I2 222. See discussion in Calder 1975 and, with texts, Siropoulos 2001, esp. 11–12.
11 *IG* XII, 3 nos. 868 and 869 [= nos. 1010 and 1695 Peek, *Griechische Verseinschriften*]; cf. Siropoulos 2001, 12. This later Admetus claims an "equal glory" (*ison kleos*, 1010 Peek, line 3) with his namesake and ancestor. He was also a priest of Carneian Apollo; one wonders if there is any link, however tenuous, with the promise at lines 448–50 that the story of Alcestis (and therefore Admetus too!) will be hymned at Sparta in the "Carneian month."
12 Valerius Maximus, writing a collection of *Memorable Doings and Sayings* in the early Roman empire, speaks of Alcestis' voluntary death (*voluntario obitu*, 4. 6. 1) but says Admetus was condemned (*damnatum*) for allowing it. It is a rare explicit criticism and is curiously out of place in the text; Valerius regularly gathers together Roman examples on a topic (in this case "on conjugal love"), followed by a separate section of external or foreign examples. Here the Greek example of Alcestis and Admetus intrudes into the Roman list, and one wonders if a later reader's argumentative marginal note might have crept into Valerius' text.

13 Wood 1978, esp. 499–505 and fig. 1. Discussed and illustrated in *LIMC* s.v. Alkestis nos. 8 (death of Alcestis) and 16 (return and remarriage), with plates.
14 Wood 1978, 509–10, fig. 7; *LIMC* s.v. Alkestis no. 13, with plate.
15 Tomb of Vincentius and Vibia: *LIMC* s.v. Alkestis no. 50, with plate; tomb of the Nasones: *LIMC* s.v. Alkestis no. 51, with drawing.
16 Berg 1994, 222; *LIMC* s.v. Alkestis no. 24, with plate. The lost tomb of the Nasones in the second century AD also showed Alcestis' return by Heracles to a seated Admetus: *LIMC* s.v. Alkestis no. 25, with drawing.
17 Text and English translation with commentary in Marcovich 1988.
18 I am grateful to my colleague David Bright for much help and access to his unpublished work on the poem. See also Hall 2008.
19 While gaps remain in the text, some assume the poem is essentially complete as we have it. Even though narrative plays a surprisingly small part in the overall composition, it still seems very abrupt to end with Alcestis' cry that "The infernal god is wrapping my limbs in sleep," without any narrative conclusion. It seems much more likely that the original ending has been lost.
20 Kolve 1981, esp. 242–3nn. 51, 54.
21 "Hast thou not in a book, li'th in thy chest,
The greate goodness of the queen Alceste,
That turned was into a daisy
She that for her husbande chose to die,
And eke to go to hell rather than he;
And Hercules rescued her, pardie!
And brought her out of hell again to bliss?"
And I answer'd again, and saide; "Yes,
Now know I her; and is this good Alceste,
The daisy, and mine own hearte's rest?" (498–504)
22 Kolve 1981, 173–8.
23 Wilson 1984. Much more skeptical is Parker 2007, xxvii–xxviii.
24 For text and brief discussion, see Hughes 1967, 170–1.
25 Propertius 4.11.73ff. ("I commend our children to you as shared pledges," *commendo communia pignora natos*); see the commentary of Austin 1964, 285 *ad* 789 and Euripides, *Alcestis* 377 ("become

now a mother to these children in place of me"). One wonders if Milton saw Alcestis behind Vergil's Creusa. See further Slater 2007 [2009].

26 Exactly the same three lines describe Aeneas' futile attempt to embrace his deceased father Anchises in the underworld (*Aeneid* 6, 700–2), and for the reader who sees the ghost of Creusa in Book 2, appearing in a cityscape more hellish than most of the underworld vision of Book 6, a despairing tone is not far to seek.
27 Though there are considerable differences from Euripides in Quinault's libretto: comparative synopses in Thorp 2010, 93; cf. Parker 2007, xxix, with further references.
28 For a detailed, though hardly dispassionate, account of the transformations of the Alcestis theme from the seventeenth to twentieth centuries, see Butler 1937.
29 Sternfeld 1966, esp. 123.
30 Wygant 2010, esp. 106.
31 Racine is answering a critic who tried to defend the libretto of Lully's opera by disparaging Euripides. For more details and the place of this dispute in the developing "Quarrel of the Ancients and the Moderns," see Parker 2007, xxxvi–xxxviii.
32 See the "Translator's" note in Alfieri 1957, 1205–9 (play text, 1157–204). The English translation of Lloyd in Bowring 1876 (reprinted 1970) lacks this note.
33 I know of no direct evidence that Verrall knew Alfieri's version, but there is a notable similarity to his explanation of Alcestis' resurrection: see below, 85–6.
34 Text and translation in Stern 1996.
35 Details in Hall and Macintosh 2005, 433–6, along with other burlesques.
36 Hall and Macintosh 2005, 438–42, esp. 441. Leighton's painting is now in the Wadsworth Athenaeum, Hartford, Conn.
37 Hall and Macintosh 2005, 250–5; 255.
38 Easterling 1999, 30.
39 See the story in Beard 2000, 47–50.
40 Pluggé 1938, 14.

41 I cite Browning's text from Pettigrew 1981. A brief critical appreciation can be found in Hall and Macintosh 2005, 442–4.
42 Balaustion's Adventure 206–8. The word is used by Dioscurides and Galen, but the grounds for Browning's use of it as a name are not clear.
43 Brown 2009, 293–5. Hall and Macintosh (2005, 444) see her as both Alcestis and Balaustion.
44 E.g. 711 and, more forcefully, 714–16: "(Also Euripides saw plain enough: / But you and I, Charopé!—you and I / Will trust his sight until our own grow clear.)"
45 Verrall 1895, 77–8.
46 Murray (1960, 149–75) includes Sybil Thorndyke's reminiscences of Murray and her performances in his translations; cf. West 1984, 88–104; Wilson 1987, 195–200. For a critical assessment of the translations see Morwood 2007.
47 Murray 1960, 155–7 (and, with a photo of Barker in the role, Kennedy 1985, 68–9). A young Barker was apparently the first to suggest to Murray that his translations, originally written for a reading public, could be staged. Barker mounted a series of professional productions in Britain, beginning with the *Hippolytus* in 1904, and hoped to direct *Alcestis* but, after his 1915 American tour, never returned to Euripides.
48 "Euripides and Professor Murray," 1918, republished in Eliot 1932, 46–50.
49 Nor is the feeling now confined to those who have read Verrall. Dale (1954, xxiv), discussing reactions to the character of Admetus, goes on to point out "Alcestis … is a more awkward problem … and it is usually left to young readers to voice a more open disappointment. She should not sing her own praises so loudly, they feel, and they remain unconvinced even when told that this was not considered such bad form in ancient Greece."
50 Eliot 1950.
51 Eliot 1951, 38 [= 1957, 91].
52 Heilman 1953; Reckford 1964; Most 2010, 109.
53 Reckford (1991) also hears echoes of Plato's *Symposium* in Eliot's play, including themes of moral growth through love.
54 See the Forward by his sister, Isabel Wilder, published in Wilder 1977.

55 Wilder 1977, 57.
56 Wilder 1977, 98.
57 For a more positive assessment, see Koutsoudaki 1994.
58 Hughes 1999. The script has been produced by Barry Rutter of the Northern Broadsides Theatre Company in Halifax, UK (see the timeline of Hughes' career compiled by Ann Skea at: http://www.zeta.org.au/~annskea/timeline.htm) and by BBC Radio 3 (November 2001).
59 The impulse to import other material into the *Alcestis* is notable in other twentieth-century stagings. Although the performance script has never been published, Robert Wilson mounted a famous *Alcestis* at the American Repertory Theater in Cambridge, Massachusetts, in 1986, which combined a translation by Dudley Fitts and Robert Fitzgerald with German and Japanese Kyogen sources: documentation in Fuchs 1986; her original *Village Voice* review is reprinted in Fuchs 1996.
60 Marshall 2009.
61 Hughes 1999, 1.
62 Hughes 1999, 4.
63 Hughes 1999, 13.
64 Hughes 1999, 29.
65 See Marshall 2009, 275–6, with further references.
66 Hughes 1999, 70.
67 Hughes 1999, 81.
68 Hughes 1999, 102.
69 Elaine Connell, review, September 22, 2000 at: http://www.mytholmroyd.net/tedhughes/alcestis2.html. The lines quoted are the chorus' last three lines, split between two speakers (Hughes 1999, 103).

Bibliography

V. Alfieri, *Le Tragedie*, ed. P. Cazzani (Milan: A. Mondadori, 1957).

W. G. Arnott, *Alexis: The Fragments* (Cambridge: Cambridge University Press, 1996).

R. G. Austin, *P. Vergili Maronis Aeneidos Liber Secundus* (Oxford: Clarendon Press, 1964).

K. Bassi, "The Actor as Actress in Euripides' *Alcestis*," *Themes in Drama* 11 (1989) pp. 19–30.

M. Beard, *The Invention of Jane Harrison* (Cambridge, MA: Harvard University Press, 2000).

E. Belfiore, *Murder among Friends: Violation of Philia in Greek Tragedy* (New York: Oxford University Press, 2000).

J. M. Bell, "Euripides' *Alkestis*: A Reading," *Emerita* 48 (1980) pp. 43–75.

B. Berg, "Alcestis and Hercules in the Catacomb of Via Latina," *Vigiliae Christianae* 48 (1994) pp. 219–34.

G. G. Betts, "The Silence of Alcestis," *Mnemosyne* 18 (1965) pp. 181–2.

C. R. Beye, "Alcestis and Her Critics," *Greek, Roman, and Byzantine Studies* 2 (1959) pp. 109–27.

E. A. Bowring (ed.), *The Tragedies of Vittorio Alfieri*, trans. C. Lloyd, 2 vols (Westport, CT: Greenwood Press, 1970).

D. W. Bradeen, "The Athenian Casualty Lists," *Classical Quarterly* 19 (1969) pp. 145–59.

E. M. Bradley, "Admetus and the Triumph of Failure in Euripides' *Alcestis*," *Ramus* 9 (1980) pp. 112–27.

S. A. Brown, "Classics Reanimated: Ted Hughes and Reflexive Translation," in R. Rees (ed.), *Ted Hughes and the Classics* (Oxford: Oxford University Press, 2009) pp. 282–99.

A. P. Burnett, "The Virtues of Admetus," *Classical Philology* 60 (1965) pp. 240–55.

—*Catastrophe Survived* (Oxford: Oxford University Press, 1971).

E. M. Butler, "Alkestis in Modern Dress," *Journal of the Warburg Institute* 1 (1937) pp. 46–60.

R. Buxton, "Euripides' *Alkestis*: Five Aspects of an Interpretation," in
J. Mossman (ed.), *Euripides* (Oxford: Oxford University Press, 2003)
pp. 170–86 [= in L. Rodley (ed.), *Papers Given at a Colloquium in
Honour of R. P. Winnington Ingram* (London, 1987) pp. 17–31].

W. M. Calder, "The Alkestis Inscription from Odessos: IGBR I2 222,"
American Journal of Archaeology 79 (1975) pp. 80–83.

V. Castellani, "Notes on the Structure of Euripides' *Alcestis*," *American
Journal of Philology* 100 (1979) pp. 487–96.

S. Cavell, *Pursuits of Happiness: the Hollywood Comedy of Remarriage*
(Cambridge, MA: Harvard University Press, 1981).

C. Clairmont, *Patrios Nomos: Public Burial in Athens during the Fifth and
Fourth Centuries B.C.*, BAR 161 (Oxford: Oxford University Press, 1983).

S. G. Cole, "Procession and Celebration at the Dionysia," in R. Scodel (ed.),
Theater and Society in the Classical World (Ann Arbor, MI: University of
Michigan Press, 1993) pp. 25–38.

C. Collard, M. J. Cropp, and K. H. Lee, *Euripides: Selected Fragmentary
Plays*, Volume I (Warminster: Aris and Phillips, 1995).

E. Csapo, "The Men Who Built the Theatres: *Theatropolai*, *Theatronai*,
and *Arkhitektones*," in P. Wilson (ed.), *The Greek Theatre and Festivals.
Documentary Studies. Oxford Studies in Ancient Documents* (Oxford:
Oxford University Press, 2007).

A. M. Dale (ed.), *Euripides' Alcestis* (Oxford: Oxford University Press, 1954).

J. Davidson, "Carcinus and the Temple: A Problem in the Athenian
Theater," *Classical Philology* 98 (2003) pp. 109–22.

A. A. Donohue, *Xoana and the Origins of Greek Sculpture* (Atlanta, GA:
Scholars Press, 1988).

M. Dyson, "Alcestis' Children and the Character of Admetus," *Journal of
Hellenic Studies* 108 (1988) pp. 13–23.

P. Easterling, "The Early Years of the Cambridge Greek Play: 1882–1912,"
in *Classics in 19th and 20th Century Cambridge: Curriculum, Culture
and Community*, Cambridge Philological Society Supplement 24
(Cambridge: Cambridge Philological Society, 1999) pp. 27–47.

T. S. Eliot, *Selected Essays, 1917–1932* (New York: Harcourt, 1932)
["Euripides and Professor Murray" is reprinted with the same
pagination in *Selected Essays* (New York, 1964)].

—*Poetry and Drama* (Cambridge, MA: Harvard University Press, 1951) [reprinted as Eliot's *On Poetry and Drama* (London, 1957) pp. 75–95].
H. Erbse, "Euripides' *Alcestis*," *Philologus* 116 (1972) pp. 32–52.
C. A. Faraone, *Talismans and Trojan Horses* (Oxford: Oxford University Press, 1992).
—*Ancient Greek Love Magic* (Cambridge, MA: Harvard University Press, 1999).
H. P. Foley, "*Anodos* Dramas: Euripides' *Alcestis* and *Helen*," in R. Hexter and D. Selden (eds), *Innovations of Antiquity* (New York: Routledge, 1992) pp. 133–60.
E. Fuchs (ed.), "The PAJ Casebook: Robert Wilson's *Alcestis*," *Performing Arts Journal* 28 (1986).
—*The Death of Character: Perspectives on Theater after Modernism* (Bloomington, IN: Indiana University Press, 1996).
R. Garland, *The Greek Way of Death* (Ithaca, NY: Cornell University Press, 1985).
R. Garner, "Death and Victory in Euripides' *Alcestis*," *Classical Antiquity* 7 (1988) pp. 58–71.
S. Goldhill, "The Great Dionysia and Civic Ideology," in J. J. Winkler and F. I. Zeitlin (eds), *Nothing to Do with Dionysos? Athenian Drama in its Social Context* (Princeton: Princeton University Press, 1990) pp. 97–129.
—"Civic Ideology and the Problem of Difference: The Politics of Aeschylean Tragedy, Once Again," *Journal of Hellenic Studies* 120 (2000) pp. 34–56.
J. Gregory, *Euripides and the Instruction of the Athenians* (Ann Arbor, MI: University of Michigan Press, 1991).
M. Griffith, "Brilliant Dynasts: Power and Politics in the *Oresteia*," *Classical Antiquity* 14 (1995) pp. 62–129.
E. Hall, "Is the 'Barcelona Alcestis' a Latin Pantomime Libretto?" in E. Hall and R. Wyles (eds), *New Directions in Ancient Pantomime* (Oxford and New York: Oxford University Press, 2008) pp. 258–82.
E. Hall and F. Macintosh, *Greek Tragedy and the British Theatre, 1660–1914* (Oxford and New York: Oxford University Press, 2005).
M. R. Halleran, "Alkestis Redux," *Harvard Studies in Classical Philology* 86 (1982) pp. 51–3.
K. Hartigan, *Ambiguity and Self-Deception: The Apollo and Artemis Plays*

of Euripides, Studien zur klassischen Philologie 50 (Frankfurt am Main and New York: Peter Land Pub Inc., 1991).

M. Heath, "Euripides' *Telephus*," *Classical Quarterly* 37 (1987) pp. 272–80.

R. B. Heilman, "*Alcestis* and *The Cocktail Party*," *Comparative Literature* 5 (1953) pp. 105–16.

J. Henderson, "Women and the Athenian Dramatic Festivals," *Transactions of the American Philological Association* 121 (1991) pp. 133–47.

M. Y. Hughes (ed.), *John Milton: Complete Poems and Major Prose* (Indianapolis, IN: Prentice Hall, 1967).

S. C. Humphreys, *The Family, Women, and Death*, 2nd edn (Ann Arbor, MI: Michigan University Press, 1993).

D. I. Iakov, "Euripides' *Alcestis* as Closed Drama," *Rivista di filologia e di istruzione classica* 138 (2010) pp. 14–27.

R. Kilpatrick, "'When a God Contrives:' Divine Providence in *Alcestis* and *Ajax*," *Dionysius* 10 (1986) pp. 3–20.

D. Kennedy, *Granville Barker and the Dream of Theatre* (Cambridge: Cambridge University Press, 1985).

V. A. Kolve, "From Cleopatra to Alceste: An Iconographic Study of *The Legend of Good Women*," in J. P. Herrmann and J. J. Burke (eds), *Signs and Symbols in Chaucer's Poetry* (Tuscaloosa, AL: University of Alabama Press, 1981) pp. 130–78, 233–45.

M. Koutsoudaki, "Thornton Wilder's *The Alcestiad* and Minor Plays," *Classical and Modern Literature* 14 (1994) pp. 345–59.

D. Konstan, *Friendship in the Classical World* (Cambridge: Cambridge University Press, 1997).

D. C. Kurtz, and J. Boardman, *Greek Burial Customs* (London: Thames and Hudson, 1971).

R. Lattimore, *Themes in Greek and Latin Epitaphs* (Urbana: The University of Illinois Press, 1962).

LIMC = *Lexicon Iconographicum Mythologiae Classicae* (Zurich, 1981–) 8 vols in 2 parts each. J. Boardman et al. (eds) [s.v. "Alkestis," vol. 1/1, pp. 533–44, vol. 1/2, pls., pp. 399–408].

M. Lloyd, "Euripides' *Alcestis*," *Greece & Rome* 32 (1985) pp. 119–31.

—*The Agon in Euripides* (Oxford: Oxford University Press, 1992).

N. Loraux, *The Invention of Athens: The Funeral Oration in the Classical*

City, trans. A. Sheridan (Cambridge, MA: Harvard University Press, 1986).
—*Tragic Ways of Killing a Woman*, trans. A. Forster (Cambridge, MA: Harvard University Press, 1987).
C. A. E. Luschnig, "Euripides' *Alcestis*' and the Athenian *Oikos*," *Dioniso* 60 (1990) pp. 9–39.
—"Playing the Others: The Mythological Confusions of Admetus," *Scholia* 1 (1992) pp. 12–27.
B. Lush, "Irony and the Rejection of Imagined Alternatives in Euripides' *Alcestis*," *Classical Journal* 107 (2012) pp. 385–407.
D. M. MacDowell, *The Law in Classical Athens* (Ithaca: Cornell University Press, 1978).
F. Macintosh, "Alcestis in Britain," in M.-H. Garelli-François, P. Sauzeau, and M.-P. Noël (eds), *D'un "genre" à l'autre*, Cahiers du GITA 14 (Montpellier, 2001) pp. 281–308.
M. Marcovich, *Alcestis Barcinonensis: Text and Commentary*, Mnemosyne Supplement 103 (Leiden: Brill Academic Publishers, 1988).
C. W. Marshall, "*Alcestis* and the Problem of Prosatyric Drama," *Classical Journal* 95 (2000) pp. 229–38.
—"*Alcestis* and the Ancient Rehearsal Process (P. Oxy. 4546)," *Arion* 11 (2004) pp. 27–45.
C. W. Marshall and S. van Willigenburg, "Judging Athenian dramatic competitions," *Journal of Hellenic Studies* 124 (2004) pp. 90–107.
H. Marshall, "The Hughes Version: Commercial Considerations and Dramatic Imagination," in R. Rees (ed.), *Ted Hughes and the Classics* (Oxford: Oxford University Press, 2009) pp. 263–81.
D. J. Mastronarde, "Actors on High: the Skene-Roof, the Crane, and the Gods in Attic Drama," *Classical Antiquity* 9 (1990) pp. 247–94.
C. Meier, *The Political Art of Greek Tragedy*, trans. A. Webber (Baltimore: The Johns Hopkins University Press, 1993).
E. A. Meyer, "Epitaphs and Citizenship in Classical Athens," *Journal of Hellenic Studies* 103 (1993) pp. 99–121.
A. N. Michelini, *Euripides and the Tragic Tradition* (Madison, WI: University of Wisconsin Press, 1987).

L. Mignanego, "From Shroud to Veil: A Study of the *Alcestis*," *Appunti romani di filologia* 5 (2003) pp. 41–69.

R. Mitchell-Boyask (ed.), *Approaches to Teaching the Dramas of Euripides* (New York: Modern Language Association of America, 2002).

S. Montiglio, *Silence in the Land of Logos* (Princeton: Princeton University Press, 2000).

J. Morwood, "Gilbert Murray's Translations of Greek Tragedy," in Christopher Stray (ed.), *Gilbert Murray Reassessed: Hellenism, Theatre, and International Politics* (Oxford and New York: Oxford University Press, 2007) pp. 133–44.

I. Morris, *Death-Ritual and Social Structure in Classical Antiquity* (Cambridge: Cambridge University Press, 1992).

G. Most, "*Alcestis Redux*," *New England Classical Journal* 37 (2010) pp. 99–112.

S. Murnaghan, "The Survivors' Song: The Drama of Mourning in Euripides' *Alcestis*," *Illinois Classical Studies* 24–25 (1999) pp. 107–16.

G. Murray, *Gilbert Murray: An Unfinished Autobiography* (London: Allen and Unwin, 1960).

R. M. Nielsen, "Alcestis: A Paradox in Dying," *Ramus* 5 (1976) pp. 92–102.

J. Oakley and R. Sinos, *The Wedding in Ancient Athens* (Madison, WI: University of Wisconsin Press, 1993).

D. O'Higgins, "Above Rubies: Admetus' Perfect Wife," *Arethusa* 26 (1993) pp. 77–97.

M. W. Padilla, "Gifts of Humiliation: *Charis* and Tragic Experience in *Alcestis*," *American Journal of Philology* 121 (2000) pp. 179–211.

C. B. Patterson, "Those Athenian Bastards," *Classical Antiquity* 9 (1990) pp. 40–73.

A. W. Pickard-Cambridge, *The Dramatic Festivals of Athens*, 2nd edn, rev. J. Gould and D. M. Lewis, reissued with supplement and corrections (Oxford: Oxford University Press, 1988).

D. Pluggé, *History of Greek Play Production in American Colleges and Universities from 1881 to 1936*, Contributions to Education No. 752 (New York: Teachers College, Columbia University, 1938).

D. H. Porter, "MacLeish's *Herakles* and Wilder's *Alcestiad*," *Classical Journal* 80 (1984/5) pp. 145–50.

K. J. Reckford, "Heracles and Mr. Eliot," *Comparative Literature* 16 (1964) pp. 1–18.

—"Eliot's *Cocktail Party* and Plato's *Symposium*," *Classical and Modern Literature* 11 (1991) pp. 303–12.

R. Rehm, *Marriage to Death: The Conflation of Wedding and Funeral Rituals in Greek Tragedy* (Princeton: Princeton University Press, 1994).

T. G. Rosenmeyer, "*Alcestis*: Character and Death," in *The Masks of Tragedy: Essays on Six Greek Dramas* (Austin, TX: University of Texas Press,1963) pp. 199–248.

L. Rubinstein, *Adoption in IV. Century Athens*, OGL 34 (Copenhagen: Museum Tusculanum Press, 1993).

H. Schaefer, "Das Eidolon des Leonidas," in K. Schauenberg (ed.), *Charites: Studien zur Altertumswissenschaft, Festschrift E. Langlotz* (1957) pp. 223–33.

S. L. Schein, "ΦΙΛΙΑ in Euripides' *Alcestis*," *Metis* 3 (1988) pp. 179–206.

R. Scodel, "Ἀδμήτου Λόγος and the Alcestis," *Harvard Studies in Classical Philology* 83 (1979) pp. 51–62.

R. Seaford, *Reciprocity and Ritual: Homer and Tragedy in the Developing City-State* (Oxford: Oxford University Press, 1994).

C. Segal, "Euripides' *Alcestis*: Female Death and Male Tears," *Classical Antiquity* 11 (1992) pp. 142–58.

—*Euripides and the Poetics of Sorrow* (Durham, NC, and London: Duke University Press, 1993).

H. A. Shapiro, *Personifications in Greek Art: The Representation of Abstract Concepts, 600–400 B.C.* (Zürich: Akanthus, 1993).

C. M. J. Sicking, "Admetus' Case," in *Distant Companions: Selected Papers*, Mnemosyne Supplement 185 (Leiden: Brill Academic Publishers, 1998) pp. 48–62.

G. M. Sifakis, "The Children of Greek Tragedy," *BICS* 26 (1979) pp. 67–80.

S. D. Siropoulos, "An Exemplary *Oikos*: Domestic Role-models in Euripides' *Alcestis*," *Eirene* 37 (2001) pp. 5–18.

G. Sissa, *Greek Virginity* (Cambridge, MA: Harvard University Press, 1990).

N. W. Slater, "Theozotides on Adopted Sons (Lysias fr. 6)," *Scholia* 2 (1993) pp. 82–6.

—"Waiting in the Wings: Aristophanes' *Ecclesiazusae*," *Arion* 5 (1997) pp. 97–129.

— "Dead Again: (En)gendering Praise in Euripides' *Alcestis*," *Helios* 27 (2000) pp. 105–21.

— *Spectator Politics: Metatheatre and Performance in Aristophanes* (Philadelphia, PA: University of Pennsylvania Press, 2002).

— "Some Accian Women," in S. Faller and G. Manuwald (eds), *Accius und seine Zeit*, Identitäten und Alteritäten 13 (Würzburg: Ergan Verlag, 2002) pp. 289–303.

— "Nothing to Do with Satyrs? *Alcestis* and the Concept of Prosatyric Drama," in G. W. M. Harrison (ed.), *Satyr Drama: Tragedy at Play* (Classical Press of Wales, 2006) pp. 83–101.

— "Mourning Becomes Alcestis: A Note on Milton, Sonnet 23," *Classical and Modern Literature* 27 (2007 [2009]) pp. 1–5.

G. Smith, "The *Alcestis* of Euripides: An Interpretation," *Rivista di Filologia e di Istruzione Classica* 111 (1983) pp. 129–45.

G. R. Stanton, "*Philia* and *Xenia* in Euripides' 'Alkestis'," *Hermes* 118 (1990) pp. 42–54.

J. Stern (trans.), *Palaephatus: On Unbelievable Tales* (Wauconda, IL: Bolchazy-Carducci Publishers, 1996).

F. Sternfeld, "Expression and Revision in Gluck's *Orfeo* and *Alceste*," in J. Westrup (ed.), *Essays Presented to Egon Wellesz* (Oxford: Clarendon Press, 1966) pp. 114–29.

M. Stieber, "Statuary in Euripides' *Alcestis*," *Arion* 5 (1998) pp. 69–97.

A. Suter, "Lament in Euripides' *Trojan Women*," *Mnemosyne* 16 (2003) pp. 1–28.

— "Male Lament in Greek Tragedy," in A. Suter (ed.), *Lament: Studies in the Ancient Mediterranean and Beyond* (Oxford: Oxford University Press, 2008) pp. 156–80.

J. E. Thorburn, "The Third Stasimon of Euripides' *Alcestis*," *Scripta Classica Israelica* 19 (2000) pp. 35–49.

J. Thorp, "Dance in Lully's *Alceste*," in P. Brown and S. Ograjenšek (eds), *Ancient Drama in Music for the Modern Stage* (London and New York: Oxford University Press, 2010) pp. 85–95.

E. M. Thury, "Euripides' *Alcestis* and the Athenian Generation Gap," *Arethusa* 21 (1988) pp. 197–214.

M. Toher, "On the εἴδωλον of a Spartan King," *Rheinisches Museum* 142 (1999) pp. 113–27.

E. Vermeule, *Aspects of Death in Early Greek Art and Poetry* (Berkeley: University of California Press, 1979).

J.-P. Vernant, "Figuration de l'invisible et catégorie psychologique du double: le colossus," in *Mythe et pensée chez les Grecs* (Paris: La Decouverte, 1985).

A. W. Verrall, *Euripides the Rationalist: A Study in the History of Art and Religion* (Cambridge, MA: Harvard University Press, 1895) [reprinted 1967, New York].

T. B. L. Webster, *The Tragedies of Euripides* (London: Methuen & Co. Publishers, 1967).

F. West, *Gilbert Murray: A Life* (London: Palgrave Macmillan, 1984).

D. B. Wilson, "Euripides' *Alcestis* and the Ending of Shakespeare's *The Winter's Tale*," *Iowa State Journal of Research* 58 (1984) pp. 345–55.

D. Wilson, *Gilbert Murray OM* (Oxford: Oxford University Press, 1987).

P. Wilson, *The Athenian Institution of the Khoregia: The Chorus, the City and the Stage* (Cambridge, MA: Harvard University Press, 2000).

J. J. Winkler, "The Ephebes' Song: *Tragôidia* and *Polis*," in J. J. Winkler and F. I. Zeitlin (eds), *Nothing to Do with Dionysos? Athenian Drama in Its Social Context* (Princeton: Princeton University Press, 1990).

V. Wohl, *Intimate Commerce: Exchange, Gender, and Subjectivity in Greek Tragedy* (Austin: University of Texas Press, 1998).

S. Wood, "Alcestis on Roman Sarcophagi," *American Journal of Archaeology* 82 (1978) pp. 499–510.

T. D. Woolsey, *The Alcestis of Euripides: With Notes, for the Use of Colleges in the United States* (Boston: J. Munroe, 1853).

E. S. Wright, "The Forms of Lament in Greek Tragedy" (Ph.D. dissertation, University of Pennsylvania, 1986).

A. Wygant, "The Ghost of Alcestis," in P. Brown and S. Ograjenšek (eds), *Ancient Drama in Music for the Modern Stage* (London and New York: Oxford University Press, 2010) pp. 96–111.

F. I. Zeitlin, "Playing the Other: Theater, Theatricality, and the Feminine in Greek Drama," in J. J. Winkler and F. I. Zeitlin (eds), *Nothing to Do with Dionysos? Athenian Drama in its Social Context* (Princeton: Princeton University Press, 1990) pp. 63–96.

Index

Page references in **bold** indicate a principal discussion.

Accius 69–70
actors
   appearing at Proagon 6
   child 12, 22–3
   competition for 13
   introduction of second, third 12
   scenes for three 64, 111n. 27
   see also parts
adoption 39, 55, 118n. 62
Aeneas 78–9
Aeschines 52–3
Aeschylus 1
   Eumenides 27
   Oresteia 2, 64, 90
   Persians 48, 111n. 26
   Seven Against Thebes 118n. 66
Aesclepius 18
age identity 37
agôn 26, 118n. 64
aidôs 25, 26, 63
Alfieri, Vittorio 80–1
anapaests 18, 49
Apollo 8–9, **16–17**, 25, 32, 35, 41–3, 56, 83
   Carneian 23, 122n. 11
   the Healer 19
   in Wilder's *Alcestiad* 88–90
Apollodorus 8–9, 70
arêtê 47, 114n. 22
Argo 35, 38
aristê 21, 28, **50**
Aristophanes 3, 46, 54, 65
   Birds 53
   Dionysus reading Euripides in *Frogs* 122n. 3
   parodying *Telephus* 3
   watching Euripides 3

Artemidorus 37, 113n. 17
Artemis 8–9, 35

Balaustion's Adventure *see* Browning, Robert
Barcelona Alcestis 74–5
bed **19**, 20–1, 28, 32, 57, 66, 112n. 8
betrayal 19, 109n. 10
Boccacio, Giovanni 75
bow
   of Apollo 16, 108n. 2
   of Heracles 93
bride of Death (bride of Hades) 45, 112n. 8, 121n. 88
bride theft 62
Browning, Robert 83

Callias, *Satyrs* 7
casualty lists 40, 55, 114n. 23, 117n. 60
Cerberus 28, 73, 74
change of scene 27
charis **41–5**, 67, 115n. 32
Chaucer, Geoffrey 75–6
children 19–24, 34, 36, **38–40**, 54–5
   Eumelus, Perimele 38
choregion 106n. 9
choregos 13, 105n. 2, 107n. 17
   Themistocles as, for Phrynichus' *Alcestis* 107n. 17
   of unknown Euripides play 105n. 2
chorus 14
   arrival of 17
   composed of old men 17
   decreed in honor of Alcestis' return 30, 35, 57
   departure of, during play **26–7**, 110n. 22

divided into half-choruses 17–18, 56, 118n. 66
 individual voices in 28
 numbering fifteen, 14–15
 at Proagon 6
 sings in Doric 15
Christian reception of Alcestis 73–5, 79
Cleisthenes, tribal organization under 40, 114n. 23
closure 48–9
Cocktail Party, The 86–7
comedy, Alcestis' story in 121n. 86
competition
 for actors 13
 for playwrights 12–13
 see also Dionysia
costume 16
 of Alcestis 65–6
 of Apollo 16, 108n. 2
 of Death 16
crowns 52, 116n. 52, 117n. 55

dactylics 49
daimon 29, 91, 110n. 23
death, onstage 22
Death 30, 32, 63, 83, 90, 108n. 5
 appearance of 108n. 6
 confronting Apollo **16–17**, 56, 79
 doubling with Admetus 107n. 22
 iconography of elsewhere 16–17, 108nn. 5, 6
 in Phrynichus 9
 see also bride of Death
deception 25, 29, 44, 46
decree of Morychides 6
Demosthenes, *On the Crown* 52
dextrarum junctio 63
Diagoras 53
Diomedes 24, 29, 42, 114n. 28
Dionysia, City 1–2, 117n. 54
 structure of 3–5, 12, **51–4**, 105n. 7, 111n. 27

Dionysia, Rural 106n. 12
dithyramb 4
door, as marker 28, **32–4**, 112n. 7

eccyclema 20, 109n. 11
ekphora 48
Eliot, T. S. 86–7
epitaphs 47, 71, 121n. 88
Euhodus and Metilia Acte 72
Euripides
 Alcmaeon in Psophis 2
 Andromache 22, 111n. 28, 112n. 5, 116n. 42
 Children of Heracles 34
 Cretan Women 2
 Daughters of Pelias 1
 Hecuba 111n. 26,
 Helen 3, 111n. 28, 115n. 37, 121n. 88
 Hippolytus 22, 35, 80
 Ion 115n. 37
 Iphigenia at Aulis 34, 79
 Iphigenia in Tauris 3
 Medea 12, 61, 111n. 28
 Protesilaus 119n. 68
 Suppliants 116n. 42
 Telephus 2, 3, 5, 7, 12, 105n. 5, 111n. 27
 Trojan Women 115n. 37, 118n. 66
Eurystheus 17, 24

Fates 9, 16, 36, 41, 108n. 3
 in Wilder's *Alcestiad* 90
femininity 65–6
feminization 36, 51, 56, 60, 113n. 16
festival 37, 69 see also Dionysia, City
Fulgentius 71, 75

gender reversal 39, 55, 59, 61
gender roles 36–7, 65–6
genre 31, 52, 83
gêrotrophia 39, 114n. 21
gesture 43, 63, 65, 110–11n. 25
 of adoption 118n. 62

of marriage 30, 38, 72
ghosts 30, 111n. 26
gift exchange 22, 43, 45 see also charis
Gluck, C. W. 79, 81
Goldhill, Simon 51–2, 60
goos 28, 48–9
Gower, John 76–7
guest-friendship 24–5, 30, 32, 41, 114n. 22 see also xenia

Hades 20, 23, 27, 68, 72, 109n. 12
hair, shorn for mourning 24
Harrison, Jane 82
Heracles
    actor of also playing Alcestis 107n. 26
    in ancient art 72–4
    arrival of 23–4
    as *philos* 44
    riotous behavior of 27, 57
    see also deception, guest-friendship, xenia
Hesiod, *Catalogue of Women* 8, 38, 106n. 13
Holmes, Sherlock 64
Homer
    Iliad 8, 51
    Odyssey 109n. 13, 113n. 18
hospitality *see* guest-friendship
house *see* oikos
Hughes, Ted 91–4
Hyginus 70, 75, 106n. 14, 113n. 18
hymns 49, 122n. 11
hypothesis 3–4
    of Dicaearchus 110n. 24
    second 8, 31, 82, 105n. 1, 118n. 67

iambics 20, 49
induction 15
inscriptions, funerary 47, 71, 73, 122n. 9 *see also* epitaphs
irony 47, 60–1, 63–4, 66, 85

Jason 35, 38
judges of festival competition 12, 117n. 54
Juvenal 70

kleos 49, 50, 56, 65
    female 60
kolossos 58
kommos 28, 48
kômos 7, 28
kosmos 65–6

lament 22–3, 28, 38, **47–50**, 57, 110n. 25
    full and reduced 48, 115n. 40, 116n. 42
Latin translations of *Alcestis* 77
Leighton, Frederic Lord 81–2
libations 52, 117n. 54
likeness 21 *see also* statue
lion skin 23, 74
Lully, Jean-Baptiste 79

Magna Mater 73
marriage **61–6**
    Greek conception of 24, 38, 46–7
    procession 28
    see also bed
Marshall, C. W. 6–7, 70, 107n. 22
masculinization 51, 60
masks 12–14, 64
    change of for Admetus 24
mechanê 11
metatheater 92, 111n. 27
Milton, John 78
misquotation 44
mourning 24, 27, 44
    song of 57
Murray, Gilbert 21, 86
myth, of Alcestis and Admetus **8–10**, 35–6, 67–8, 70–2, 75, 81

names, Athenian 40, 114n. 23
Nasones, Tomb of the 73

Odeon of Pericles 5–6
oikos (house) **32–4**, 39, 51, 60–1, 112n. 3
   as city 55
orchestra **11**
   arrival of chorus in 17–18, 56
   empty 26–8, 48, 57
   tribute displayed in 5, 52
orphans 5, 52, 54–5, 60, 116n. 51

P. Oxy. 4546 70, 107n. 22
paean 23
Palaephatus 81
pantomime 75
parodoi 11
parody 2–3, 46
   self parody 115n. 37
parts
   of Admetus 107n. 22
   of Alcestis 13, 64
   distribution of 2
   of Heracles 107n. 22
Pelias 35
Penelope 76, 109n. 13, 113nn. 9, 18
Persephone 9, 68, 72
Pheres 26, 32–3, 36, 39–40, 43, 45, 50, 55, 80–1, 84, 114nn. 22, 25, 118n. 64
philia **41–5**, 114n. 22, 115n. 29
Phrynichus **9**, 16–17, 106n. 15
   introduced first female character on stage 10
   lyrics of 107n. 16
Plato, *Symposium* 68, 125n. 53
Praxilla 67
prize *see* competition
Proagon 5, 105n. 7, 106n. 8
prologue **15–17,** 41, 57
Prometheus, added to Hughes' *Alcestis* 93–4
protagonist 13

Racine, Jean 79
re-performance 8, 69, 106n. 12

rehearsal 6, 106n. 9
   text for actor rehearsing Admetus 70
remarriage 29, 33, 37, 43, **61–6**, 73, 109n. 13
   as rebirth 121n. 88
ritual 18, 47–8, 58 *see also* marriage, mourning, supplication
role *see* parts

sarcophagi 71–3
satyr play **3–4**, 9–10, 49, 83, 106n. 15
   absence of 17, 31
   single performance in fourth century 106n. 11
   by Wilder 88, 90
scolion 67
sculpture, ban on funerary 117n. 60, 119n. 73 *see also* statue
Shakespeare, William
   Coriolanus 121n. 87
   Winter's Tale 77
Shaw, G. B. 86
silence 61–6, 111n. 27
skênê **11**, 16
sophistry 18, 21, 24, 46
Sophocles 1, 12, 50, 70
   Ajax 27, 51, 109n. 14, 118n. 66
   Antigone 48, 107n. 25
   Nausikaa 10
   Oedipus at Colonus 90
   Oedipus Tyrannus 31, 35, 116n. 42
   Philoctetes 51
   Tereus 35
   Women of Trachis 34
space 38
   divided 57
   gendered 36–7
   public 37, 59
Spicer, Henry 81
stage directions 17, 108n. 1
state as parent 54
statue
   of Alcestis 57–60, 92–3, 119n. 73

in Euripides, *Protesilaus* 119n. 68
see also likeness
stepmother 21
strophic pairs 18–19
suicide 50, 77
  in Sophocles' *Ajax* 109n. 14
suppliant 63–4
sword of Death 9, 16–17, 83, 107n. 16
symposium 67, 107n. 16, 107–8n. 26

Talfourd, Frank 81
tetralogy 4, 6–7, 11, 31, 49, 105n. 1
Theater of Dionysus 2, 5, 10
  seating capacity 11, 107n. 19
three actor rule 12–13
thrênos 48
tribute 5, 52, 54

veil, of Alcestis 29–30, 36–8, 61–5, 73–4, 110n. 24, 120n. 84
Vergil, *Aeneid* 9, 79
Verrall, A. W. 85–6, 124n. 33, 125n. 49
Vincentius and Vibia, Tomb of 73
violence 16, 22, 37, 51, 55
voices
  boys' 23
  characterization in 13–14, 18, 56
  voting, for contests 107n. 23 *see also* competition

Wilder, Thornton 88–91
Wollstonecraft, Mary 80

xenia **41–5**, 62, 114n. 27 *see also* hospitality

www.ingramcontent.com/pod-product-compliance
Lightning Source LLC
Chambersburg PA
CBHW051527230426
43668CB00012B/1770